BUSINESS AND LEGAL FORMS

FOR

GRAPHIC DESIGNERS

TAD CRAWFORD

AND

EVA DOMAN BRUCK

ALLWORTH PRESS, NEW YORK

Published by Allworth Press, an imprint of Allworth Communications, Inc., 10 East 23rd Street, New York, NY 10010.

Distributor to the trade in the United States and Canada: North Light Books, an imprint of F&W Publications, Inc., 1507 Dana Avenue, Cincinnati, Ohio 45207. To order additional copies of this book, call toll-free (800) 289-0963.

Book Design by Douglas Design Associates, New York, NY.

Library of Congress Catalog Card Number: 90-80447
ISBN: 0-927629-07-0

This book is designed to provide accurate and authoritative information with respect to the subject matter covered. It is sold with the understanding that the publisher is not engaged in rendering legal, accounting, or other professional services. If legal advice or other expert assistance is required, the services of a competent attorney or professional person should be sought. While every attempt is made to provide accurate information, the authors or publisher cannot be held accountable for errors or omissions.

Table of Contents

The Forms (Tear-Out Section)

A System for Success

The knowledge and use of good business practices is an essential step toward success for any professional or company, including the graphic designer and the design firm. The forms contained in this book deal with the most important business transactions that a designer or design firm is likely to undertake. At the back of the book is an extra copy of each form, perforated on 8 1/2-by-11-inch sheets, so that the designer can remove them from the book and make copies for use in his or her business. The fact that they are designed for use, and favor the designer if negotiations are necessary, give them a unique value.

The purpose of *Business and Legal Forms for Graphic Designers* is, in part, to provide information, systems, and forms that are useful to the organization and smooth functioning of the business side of the graphic design studio. It is possible to adopt (or adapt) the entire system or alter its parts to fit the particular needs of the individual studio. Each of these organizational forms can stand on its own or be used as a component of an integrated system. While an orderly system is essential to accurate record-keeping, flexibility is important to make the system responsive to changing circumstances.

Doing Business

The organization of the forms is based upon the typical chronology of events which occur in the course of doing business in the graphic design profession (with forms for the more sophisticated contracts coming last). As a starting point, the book begins with suggestions for writing a letter of interest. One example is a letter of interest arising from the initiative of the designer. The other example is a letter responding to an expression of interest from a client. Then a very detailed estimate form for clients is used to assess the time and costs that the proposed job may require. This form can serve as an internal estimating form. It may also be a document that is shared with the client or it may be used as a means of tracking the budget and time spent for ongoing projects.

Throughout the forms, by the way, there is a selective use of the words "job" and "project" because, while both words refer to the same activity, forms which the clients will never see use the word "job" and communications that the client will receive use the word "project." The slightly more formal tone that is used to communicate with clients need not appear on everyday internal forms.

Once the project has been estimated internally and fees determined, the designer is then able to draft a proposal, which the client may sign to make a binding contract. Or the project confirmation form, which is more formal, may be used once the client has approved the contract.

The credit reference form is used to ensure that an unknown client has a satisfactory history of bill paying. After this is confirmed and the client signs to commit to the project, the assignment may be considered a "job." Several steps are taken to open the system for tracking a job on its course through the studio. The job is first assigned a number via the jobs master index, then a job sheet is opened to begin the process of recording time and costs expended on the assignment. Time sheets will show staff time expended. The studio production schedule is used to deliver the job on time.

During the course of the assignment, the project status report is used to keep the client informed of the ongoing work, and the work change order form confirms changes ordered by the client. In order to gather competitive bids for components of the job that are produced outside of the studio, the estimate request form is distributed to prospective vendors. The purchase order form serves as the designer's confirmation to a vendor to supply materials or services. It may be used to contract for illustration and photographic services, but needs to be modified for such uses. Large studios use internal requisition forms as a way of efficiently managing the purchase and allocation of needed supplies.

The payables index provides a way of tracking all incoming bills as well as a system for having these bills reviewed and identified as billable or not billable. The multi-use transmittal form has been designed for maximum flexibility and ease of use. The artwork log keeps track of all materials leaving the studio and their location within the studio once they have been returned.

Billing is an extremely important task, whether done during the course of the assignment or at its completion. The billing index provides the studio with invoice numbers as well as a handy guide for reviewing the status of payments due. Two invoice forms are provided, one in a generalized outline form and the other with a more detailed and comprehensive format. Monthly billing statements and collection letters are provided in a form that can be used directly.

Contracts

The forms then shift to focus more on the contractual relationships of the firm with the outside world. Contracts with illustrators or photographers, printers, agents, lecture sponsors, and manufacturers of licensed designs are provided along with checklists for negotiating deals. Release forms are given for the use of images of models and property. A permission form to use copyrighted materials, a copyright transfer form, and a copyright registration form (Form VA) are also included.

A contract is an agreement which creates legally enforceable obligations between two or more parties. In making a contract, each party gives something of value to the other party. This is called the exchange of consideration. Consideration can take many forms, including the giving of money or an artwork or the promise to create an artwork or pay for an artwork in the future.

All contracts, whether the designer's or someone else's, can be changed. Before using the contracts in this book, the designer should consider reviewing them with his or her attorney. This gives the opportunity to learn whether local or state laws may make it worthwhile to modify any of the provisions. For example, would it be wise to include a provision for arbitration of disputes or are the local courts speedy and inexpensive to use so no arbitration provision is necessary?

The contracts must be filled out, which means that the blanks must be completed. Beyond this, however, the designer can always delete or add provisions on any contract. Deletions or additions to a contract are usually initialed in the margin by both parties. It is also a good practice to have each party initial each page of the contract except the page on which the parties sign.

The designer must ascertain that the person signing the contract has authority to do so. If the designer is dealing with a company, the company's name should be included as well as the name of the individual authorized to sign the contract and the title of that individual (or, if it isn't clear who will sign or that person has no title, the words "Authorized Signatory" can be used instead of a title).

If the designer won't meet with the other party to sign the contract, it would be wise to have that party sign the forms first. After the designer gets back the two copies of the form, they can be signed and one copy returned to the other party. As discussed in more detail under letter contracts, this has the advantage of not leaving it up to the other party to decide whether to sign and thus make a binding contract.

If additional provisions that won't fit on the contract forms should be added, simply include a provision stating, "This contract is subject to the provisions of the rider attached hereto and made a part hereof." The rider is simply another piece of paper which would be headed "Rider to the contract between _____ and _____ dated the ____ day of _____, 19____." The additional provisions are put on this sheet and both parties sign it.

Negotiation

Understanding the business concepts behind the forms is as important as using them. By knowing why a certain provision has been included and what it accomplishes, the designer is able to negotiate when faced with someone else's contract. The designer knows what is and is not desirable.

Contracts require negotiation. The forms in this book are favorable to the designer. When they are presented to a client, printer, or supplier of creative services, changes may very well be requested. The explanation in this book of how to use each form should help the designer evaluate changes which either party may want to make. The explanation should also help the designer understand what changes would be desirable in forms presented to the designer.

Keep in mind that negotiation need not be adversarial. Certainly the designer and the other party may disagree on some points, but the basic transaction is something that both want. This larger framework of agreement must be kept in mind at all times when negotiating. Of course, the designer must also know which points are nonnegotiable and be prepared to walk away from a deal if satisfaction cannot be had on these points.

When both parties have something valuable to offer each other, it should be possible for each side to come away from the negotiation feeling they have won. This win-win negotiation requires each side to make certain that the basic needs of both parties are met so that the result is fair. The designer can't negotiate for the other side, but a wise negotiation strategy must allow the other side to meet their vital needs within the larger context which also allows the designer to obtain what he or she must have.

It is a necessity to evaluate negotiating goals and strategy before conducting any negotiations. The designer should write down what he or she must have and what can be conceded or modified. The designer should try to imagine how the shape of the contract will affect the future business relationship with the other party. Will it probably lead to success for both sides and more business or will it fail to achieve what one side or the other desires?

When negotiating, the designer should keep written notes close at hand as to goals and strategy. Notes should be kept on the negotiations too, since many conversations may be necessary before final agreement is reached. At certain points the designer should compare where the negotiations have gone with the original goals. This will help evaluate whether the designer is conducting the negotiations according to plan.

Most negotiations are done over the telephone. This makes the telephone a tool to be used wisely in negotiations. The designer should decide when he or she wants to speak with the other party. Before calling, the designer should review the notes and be familiar with the points to be negotiated. If the designer wants the other party to call, the file should be kept close at hand so there is no question as to where the negotiations stand when the call comes. If the designer is unprepared to negotiate when the other side calls, the only wise course is to call back. Negotiation demands the fullest attention and complete readiness on the part of the designer.

Oral Contracts

Despite all the forms in this book being written, it is worth addressing the question of oral contracts. There are certain contracts which must be written, such as a contract for services which will take more than one year to perform, a contract to transfer an exclusive right of copyright (an exclusive right means that no one else can do what the person receiving that right of copyright can do), or in many cases a contract for the sale of goods worth more than $500. So, without delving into the full complexity of this subject, certain contracts can be oral. If the designer is faced with a party who has breached an oral contract, an attorney should certainly be consulted for advice. The designer should not give up simply because the contract was oral.

However, while some oral contracts are valid, a written contract is always best. Even people with the most scrupulous intentions do not always remember exactly what was said or whether a particular point was covered. Disputes, and litigation, are far more likely when a contract is oral rather than written. That is another reason to make the use of written forms, like those in this book, an integral part of the business practices of any designer whose work may someday have value.

Letter Contracts

If the designer feels sending a well-drafted form will be daunting to the other party, it is always possible to adopt the more informal approach of a letter which is signed by both parties. In this case, the contracts in this book will serve as valuable checklists for the content and negotiation of the letter contract. The last paragraph of the letter would say, "If the foregoing meets with your approval, please sign both copies of this letter beneath the words AGREED TO to make this a binding contract between us." At the bottom of the letter would be the words AGREED TO with the name of the other party so he or she can sign. Again, if the other party is a company, the company name would be placed beneath the words AGREED TO as well as the name of the individual who will sign and that individual's title. This would appear as follows:

AGREED TO:
XYZ Corporation

By:_____
　　　Alice Hall, Vice President

Two copies of this letter are sent to the other party who is instructed to sign both copies and return one copy to the designer for his or her files. To be cautious, the designer can send the letters unsigned and ask the other party to sign and return both copies at which time the designer will sign and return one copy to the other party. This gives the other party an opportunity to review the final draft, but avoids a situation in which the other party might choose to delay signing and the designer would not be able to offer a similar contract to another party because the first contract might still be signed.

If the designer should ever sign a contract which the other party does not sign and return, it should be remembered that any offer to enter into a contract can always be revoked up until the time that the contract is actually entered into. The designer can protect his or her position by being the one who is last to sign, by insisting that both parties meet to sign, or by stating in the letter a deadline by which the other party must sign.

Standard Provisions

The contracts in this book contain a number of standard provisions, called "boilerplate" by lawyers. These provisions are important, although they will not seem as exciting as the provisions which relate more directly to the designer and the design process. Since these provisions can be used in almost every contract and appear in a number of the contracts in this book, an explanation of each of the provisions is given here.

Amendment. Any amendment of this Agreement must be in writing and signed by both parties.

This guarantees that any changes the parties want will be made in writing. It avoids the possibility of one party relying on oral changes to the agreement. Courts, by the way, will rarely change a written contract based on testimony that there was an oral amendment of the contract.

Arbitration. All disputes arising under this Agreement shall be submitted to binding arbitration before _____ in the following location _____ and shall be settled in accordance with the rules of the American Arbitration Association. Judgment upon the arbitration award may be entered in any court having jurisdiction thereof. Notwithstanding the foregoing, either party may refuse to arbitrate when the dispute is for a sum of less than $_____.

Arbitration can offer a quicker and less expensive way to settle disputes than litigation. However, the designer would be wise to consult a local attorney and make sure this is wise in the jurisdiction where the lawsuit would be likely to take place. The arbitrator could be the American Arbitration Association or some other person or group that both parties trust. The designer would also want the arbitration to take place where he or she is located. If small claims court is easy to use in the jurisdiction where the designer would have to sue, it might be best to have the right not to arbitrate if the disputed amount is small enough to be brought into the small claims court. In this case, the designer would put the maximum amount that can be sued for in small claims court in the space at the end of the paragraph.

Assignment. This Agreement shall not be assigned by either party hereto, provided that the Designer shall have the right to assign monies due to the Designer hereunder.

By not allowing the assignment of a contract, both parties remain more certain with whom they are dealing. Of course, a company may be purchased by new owners. If the designer only wanted to do business with the people who owned the company when the contract was entered into, change of ownership might be stated as a ground for termination in the contract. On the other hand, money is impersonal and there is no reason why the designer should not be able to assign the right to receive money.

Bankruptcy or Insolvency. If the Client shall become insolvent or if a petition in bankruptcy is filed against the Client or a Receiver or Trustee is appointed for any of the Client's assets or property, or if a lien or attachment is obtained against any of the Client's assets, this Agreement shall immediately terminate and the Client shall return to the Designer all of the Designer's work which is in the Client's possession and grant, convey, and transfer all rights in the work back to the Designer.

This provision seeks to lessen the impact on the designer of a client's bankruptcy. While the designer may lose fees, at least the work and rights may be returned. Such a provision should also appear in a publishing or licensing contract. However, the bankruptcy law may impede the provision's effectiveness.

Complete Understanding. This Agreement constitutes the entire and complete understanding between the parties hereto, and no obligation, undertaking, warranty, representation, or covenant of any kind or nature has been made by either party to the other to induce the making of this Agreement, except as is expressly set forth herein.

This provision is intended to prevent either party from later claiming that any promises or obligations exist except those shown in the written contract. A shorter way to say this is, "This Agreement constitutes the entire understanding between the parties hereto."

Cumulative Rights. All rights, remedies, obligations, undertakings, warranties, representations, and covenants contained herein shall be cumulative and none of them shall be in limitation of any other right, remedy, obligation, undertaking, warranty, representation, or covenant of either party.

This means that a benefit or obligation under one provision will not be made less because of a different benefit or obligation under another provision of the contract.

Death or Disability. In the event of the Designer's death or an incapacity of the Designer making completion of the work impossible, this Agreement shall terminate.

A provision of this kind leaves a great deal to be determined. Will payments already made be kept by the designer or the designer's estate? And who will own the work in whatever stage of completion has been reached? These issues are best resolved when the contract is negotiated.

Force Majeure. If either party hereto is unable to perform any of its obligations hereunder by reason of fire or other casualty, strike, act or order of a public authority, act of God, or other cause beyond the control of such party, then such party shall be excused from such performance during the pendancy of such cause. In the event such inability to perform shall continue longer than ____ days, either party may terminate this Agreement by giving written notice to the other party.

This provision covers events beyond the control of the parties, such as a tidal wave or a war. Certainly the time to perform the contract should be extended in such an event. There may be an issue as to how long an extension will be allowed. Also, if work has commenced and some payments have been made, the contract should cover what happens in the event of termination. Must the payments be returned? And who owns the partially completed work?

Governing Law. This Agreement shall be governed by the laws of the State of _____.

Usually the designer would want the laws of his or her own state to govern the agreement.

Liquidated Damages. In the event of the failure of XYZ Corporation to deliver by the due date, the agreed upon damages shall be $ _____ for each day after the due date until delivery takes place, provided the amount of damages shall not exceed $_____.

Liquidated damages are an attempt to anticipate in the contract what damages will be caused by a breach of the contract. Such liquidated damages must be reasonable. If they are not, they will be considered a penalty and unenforceable.

Modification. This Agreement cannot be changed, modified, or discharged, in whole or in part, except by an instrument in writing, signed by the party against whom enforcment of any change, modification, or discharge is sought.

This requires that a change in the contract must at least be written and signed by the party against whom the change will be enforced. This provision should be compared to that for amendments which requires any modification to be in writing and signed by both parties. At the least, however, this provision explicitly avoids a claim that an oral modification has been made of a written contract. Courts will almost invariably give greater weight to a written document than to testimony about oral agreements.

Notices and Changes of Address. All notices shall be sent to the Designer at the following address: _____ and to the Purchaser at the following address: _____. Each party shall be given written notification of any change of address prior to the date of said change.

Contracts often require the giving of notice. This provision facilitates giving notice by providing correct addresses and requiring notification of any change of address.

Successors and Assigns. This Agreement shall be binding upon and inure to the benefit of the parties hereto and their respective heirs, executors, administrators, successors, and assigns.

This makes the contract binding on anyone who takes the place of one of the parties, whether due to death or simply an assignment of the contract. With commissioned works, death or disability of the designer can raise complex questions about completion and ownership of the art. The issues must be resolved in the contract. Note the standard provision on assignment in fact does not allow assignment, but that provision could always be modified in the original contract or by a later written, signed amendment to the contract.

Time. Time is of the essence.

This requires each party to perform exactly to whatever time commitments they have made or be in breach of the contract. It is not a wise provision for the designer to agree to, since being a few days late in performance could cause the loss of all benefits under the contract.

Waivers. No waiver by either party of any of the terms or conditions of this Agreement shall be deemed or construed to be a waiver of such term or condition for the future, or of any subsequent breach thereof.

This means that if one party waives a right under the contract, that party has not waived the right forever and can demand that the other party perform at the next opportunity. So the designer who allowed a client not to pay on time would still have the right to demand payment. And if the client breached the contract in some other way, such as not returning original art, the fact the designer allowed this once would not prevent the designer from suing for such a breach in the future.

Warranty and Indemnity. The Designer hereby warrants that he or she is the sole creator of the Work and owns all rights granted under this Agreement. The Designer agrees to indemnify and hold harmless the Client from any and all claims, demands, payments, expenses, legal fees or other costs based on an actual breach of the foregoing warranties.

This provision protects one party against damaging actions that may have been taken by the other party. Often, one party will warrant that something is true and then indemnify and hold the other party harmless in the event that is not true. For example, a designer selling an illustration may be asked to warrant that the illustration is not plagiarized. Or the designer may ask an illustrator to warrant this to the designer. If, in fact, the illustration has been plagiarized, this would breach the warranty. The party breaching the warranty would be obligated to protect the other party who has been injured by the warranty not being true.

Volunteer Lawyers for the Arts

There are now volunteer lawyers for the arts across the nation. These groups provide free assistance to designers below certain income levels and can be a valuable source of information. To find the location of the closest volunteer lawyers for the arts group, one of the groups listed here can be contacted:

California: California Lawyers for the Arts, Fort Mason Center, Building C, Room 255, San Francisco, California 94123, (415) 775-7200; and 315 West 9th Street, Suite 1101, Los Angeles, California 90015, (213) 623-8811.

Illinois: Lawyers for the Creative Arts, 213 West Institute Place, Suite 411, Chicago, Illinois 60610, (312) 944-2787.

New York: Volunteer Lawyers for the Arts, 1285 Avenue of the Americas New York, New York 10019, (212) 977-9270.

Helpful handbooks covering the legal issues which designers face are *Legal Guide for the Visual Artist* by Tad Crawford and *Make It Legal* by Lee Wilson (both books are published by Allworth Press and distributed by North Light Books).

Graphic Arts Organizations

Belonging to an organization with fellow professionals can be important step in learning proper business practices and advancing the designer's career. The following organizations are national and well worth joining:

The American Institute of Graphic Arts (AIGA), 1059 Third Avenue, New York, New York 10021. Founded in 1914, AIGA conducts a nationwide program to promote excellence in, and the advancement of, graphic design. AIGA sponsors competitions, exhibitions, publications (including an annual, a quarterly journal, a code of ethics, professional practice guidelines, and a sales tax document), educational activities, and projects in the public interest. AIGA has chapters in a number of cities.

The Graphic Artists Guild (GAG), 11 West 20th Street, New York, New York 10011. The Guild represents 5,000 professional artists active in illustration, graphic design, textile and needle-art design, computer graphics, and cartooning. Its purposes include: to establish and promote ethical and financial standards, to gain recognition for the graphic arts as a profession, to educate members in business skills, and to lobby for artists' rights legislation. Programs include: group health insurance, monthly newsletters, publication of the landmark *Pricing and Ethical Guidelines*, legal and accounting referrals, and artist-to-artist networking and information sharing. The Guild has many local chapters across the country.

Using the Checklists

Having reviewed the basics of dealing with the business and legal forms, it is time to move on to the forms themselves and the checklists which will make the forms most useful.

These checklists focus on the key points to be observed when using the forms. On the organizational forms, the boxes can be checked when the different aspects of the use of the form have been considered. For the contracts, the checklists cover all the points which may be negotiated, whether or not they are in the contract. When, in fact, a point is covered in the contract already, the appropriate paragraph is indicated in the checklist. These checklists are especially valuable to use when reviewing a contract offered to the designer by someone else.

For the contracts, if the designer is providing the form, the boxes can be checked to be certain all the important points are covered. If the designer is reviewing someone else's form, checking the boxes will show which points they have covered and which points may have to be altered or added. By using the paragraph numbers in the checklist, the other party's provision can be quickly compared with a provision that would favor the designer. Each checklist for a contract concludes with the suggestion that the standard provisions be reviewed to see if any should be added to what the form provides. Of course, the designer does not have to include every point on the checklist in a contract, but being aware of these points will be helpful.

Code of Ethics of the AIGA

The Code of Ethics is reproduced here by permission of the AIGA. For a business system to be of value, it must encompass principles of ethics as well as efficiency.

The American Institute of Graphic Arts

Introduction to the Code of Ethics and Professional Conduct

The concept of professionalism implies a dedication to learned and uncompromised professional judgment above all other motivations. Graphic Design is still a very young profession, and it is hoped that the introduction of this document will encourage members to act cohesively to reinforce their professional status.

We ask you to read this code carefully and to use its principles to govern your professional activities. We ask that you bring it to the attention of not only your colleagues but also your students, your clients, and the public. We intend it to be a statement of what the public may expect of designers, what designers may expect of each other, and to affirm our resolve to uphold the highest levels of professional responsibility.

Acknowledgement

This document is based on the *Code of Ethics and Professional Conduct* published by the International Council of Graphic Design Associations (Icograda). The AIGA code is intended to conform with the Icograda code, while at the same time clarifying its meaning and content in the context of U.S. practice.

Purpose

The purpose of this code is to provide all AIGA members with an accepted standard of ethics and professional conduct. It presents guidelines for the voluntary conduct of members in fulfilling their professional obligations.

For the purposes of this code the word "Designer" means an individual, practicing design as a freelance or salaried graphic designer, or group of designers acting in partnership or other form of association.

The Designer's Professional Responsibility

1.1 A designer shall at all times act in a way which supports the aims of the AIGA and its members, and encourages the highest standards of design and professionalism.

1.2 A designer shall not undertake, within the context of his or her professional practice, any activity that will compromise his or her status as a professional consultant.

The Designer's Responsibility to Clients

2.1 A designer shall act in the client's best interests within the limits of professional responsibility.

2.2 A designer shall not work simultaneously on assignments which create a conflict of interest without the agreement of the clients or employers concerned, except in specific cases where it is the convention of a particular trade for a designer to work at the same time for various competitors.

2.3 A designer shall treat all work in progress prior to the completion of a project and all knowledge of a client's intentions, production methods and business organization as confidential and shall not divulge such information in any manner whatsoever without the consent of the client. It is the designer's responsibility to ensure that all staff members act accordingly.

The Designer's Responsibility to Other Designers

3.1 Designers in pursuit of business opportunities should support fair and open competition based upon professional merit.

3.2 A designer shall not knowingly accept any professional assignment on which another designer has been or is working without notifying the other designer or until he or she is satisfied that any previous appointments have been properly terminated and that all materials relevant to the continuation of the project are the clear property of the client.

3.3 A designer must not attempt, directly or indirectly, to supplant another designer; nor must he or she compete with another designer by means of unethical inducements.

3.4 A designer must be fair in criticism and shall not inaccurately denigrate the work or reputation of a fellow designer.

3.5 A designer shall not accept instructions from a client which involve infringement of another person's property rights without permission, or consciously act in any manner involving any such infringement.

3.6 A designer working in a country other than his or her own shall observe the relevant Code of Conduct of the national society concerned.

Fees

4.1 A designer shall not undertake any work for a client without adequate compensation, except with respect to work for charitable or non-profit organizations.

4.2 A designer shall not undertake any speculative projects either alone or in competition with other designers for which compensation will only be received if a design is accepted or used. This applies not only to entire projects but also to preliminary schematic proposals.

4.3 A designer may take part in any open or limited competition for work whose terms are approved by the AIGA.

4.4 A designer shall work only for a fee, a royalty, salary or other agreed upon form of compensation. A designer shall not retain any kickbacks, hidden discounts, commission, allowances or payment in kind from contractors or suppliers.

4.5 A reasonable handling and administration charge may be added, with the knowledge and understanding of the client, as a percentage to all reimbursable items, billable to a client, that pass through the designer's account.

4.6 A designer who is financially concerned with any suppliers which may benefit from any recommendations made by the designer in the course of a project shall secure the approval of the client or employer of this fact in advance.

4.7 A designer who is asked to advise on the selection of designers or other consultants shall accept no payment in any form from the designers or consultants recommended.

Publicity

5.1 Any self-promotion, advertising, or publicity must not contain deliberate misstatements of competence, experience or professional capabilities. It must be fair both to clients and other designers.

5.2 A designer may allow a client to use his or her name for the promotion of work designed or services provided but only in a manner which is appropriate to the status of the profession.

Authorship

6.1 A designer shall not claim sole credit for a design on which other designers have collaborated.

6.2 When not the sole author of a design, it is incumbent upon the designer or design firm to clearly identify their specific responsibilities or involvement with the design. Examples of such work may not be used for publicity, display or portfolio samples without clear identification of precise areas of authorship.

Notes on the Code

The wording of the code was developed to be as clear and unambiguous as possible. There are, however, certain specific instances of accepted practice which differ from general principles. These have been referred to in the relevant clauses:

Clause 2.2: It is the designer's responsibility to point out and resolve any problems arising from working simultaneously for clients who are in direct commercial competition. It may, of course, be necessary for a designer to decline commissions if such a conflict cannot be resolved. Some examples of work that is excluded because of trade conventions are books, book jackets, and record jackets.

Clause 4.1 and 4.2: The purpose of these two clauses is to encourage a level of compensation conducive to competent performance, to strengthen members' resolve to insist upon an adequate financial reward for their services, and to discourage the unfair manipulation of members into providing free services with the hope of gaining a commission. The correct course of action for a client who wishes to evaluate the specific concepts of competing designers is to evaluate the potential firms by means of interviews, select those designers in which they are interested, and pay each full fees for a schematic presentation prior to proceeding with a commission to the successful competitor. In the event that any member is approached to undertake speculative work, the proposal should be declined and the above procedure suggested.

Letter of Interest

A letter of interest can be either a response or an inquiry, depending upon who initiates the communication. When a potential client asks to see the designer's portfolio, specific samples of work, or other promotional material, a letter of interest such as Sample A acts as a cover letter or transmittal form—but with a more personal touch. When the designer is seeking work, a letter of interest such as Sample B may serve as an introduction or as a reminder that the designer and client have had previous contact.

Checklist

❑ Make sure the name, title, and address of the contact is correct in form and spelling.

❑ Avoid sounding too familiar. Use first names in the salutation only if the person is truly an acquaintance.

❑ Mention the source of information about the contact or prospective assignment, the context in which the initial contact, if any, was made; or the person, if known to the contact, who recommended this communication.

❑ Keep these letters brief, simple, and straight-forward. One page is ideal.

❑ If scheduling time is an issue, indicate availability as well as any restrictions.

❑ Sign off with a phrase that leads to the possibility of a dialogue, such as: "I would be pleased to discuss this project further;" "Let me know if I can provide you with additional material or information." "If you have any questions or concerns, please let me know so that we may discuss them."

❑ All correspondence should be on letterhead. If this is not possible, it is imperative to include the address and phone number that can be used to reach the designer.

❑ A transmittal form may take the place of a letter of interest when the prospective client requests samples or other promotional material for file purposes only. (See Transmittal Form, pages 55-56.)

Sample A. **Letter of Interest in Response to a Prospective Client**

Contact Person's Name   Date
Contact Person's Title
Client Company Name
Address

Dear

I was very pleased to hear from you (last week; yesterday; on May 2nd, etc.). Here (is; are) (my portfolio; some promotional pieces) which you requested that I send you for review.

I am seriously interested in the possibility of working on the assignment we discussed and am available to do new work (for the next __ weeks; until Thanksgiving; after New Year's; anytime in the near future).

Let me know if I can provide you with additional material or more information.

I look forward to hearing from you.

Sincerely yours,

Sample B. Letter of Interest with Designer Initiating Contact

Date

Contact Person's Name
Contact Person's Title
Client Company Name
Address

Dear

(Sample Introductions)
   I enjoyed meeting you at...
   I enjoyed hearing you talk about..., at ...
   It was a pleasure having a chance to talk with you at...
   Our mutual (friend; acquaintance; colleague), (person's name), suggested I contact you.
   I read with great interest in yesterday's newspaper (or name of magazine, etc.) about the recent developments in your firm and thought this might be an appropriate time to contact you.
   I admire the (products; services; etc.) produced by your firm and because of the nature and quality of my work, thought you might be interested in seeing some of the enclosed material.

I am seriously interested in the possibility of working with you and am available to talk at your earliest convenience.

Please feel free to let me know if there is any additional material or more information that I could provide.

I look forward to hearing from you.

Sincerely yours,

Estimate Form for Client; Preliminary Budget and Schedule; Budget and Schedule Review

The inclusion or deletion of appropriate column headings makes this a form that can serve many purposes. In the earliest stages of planning an assignment the Preliminary Budget and Schedule is used by the designer to help determine fee amounts, production costs, and the approximate amount of time needed for each phase of the job. By breaking down every aspect of the project into its separate components, the designer can more easily determine how the complexity and scale of the job will affect each task.

As the Estimate Form for Clients it outlines, item by item, how much the project will cost and how long it will take to do individual tasks. It is particularly useful to include the language indicated at the bottom of this form to assure that the client recognizes that this is an estimate and not a contract.

As the Budget and Schedule Review, this form may be used internally to track how much time and money have already been expended on specific job components and how much is left in the budget to complete the job. It may also be shared with the client at periodic intervals, in particular when budgetary problems arise from unexpected additions and changes by the client. It is advisable, however, to use considerable discretion in revealing internal financial information to clients, especially concerning the cost of design and production time when billing is rendered on a flat fee basis.

Filling in the Form

Depending upon its intended use, check the appropriate box for the preferred title of the form. Fill in the name of the client, the project, the date and the project (job) number.

For use as either an Estimate Form for Client or as a Preliminary Budget and Schedule, fill in the "allocated" column for time schedule and the "budget" column under the category of money. Delete or leave blank the columns marked "used," "spent," and "balance." For use as a Budget and Schedule Review, either internally or for client use, fill in all of the necessary information in the spaces provided. The preparer of this form should sign it in the space next to "by."

Using the Form

❑ Long term, complicated projects should be tracked periodically to make sure that time and expenses are not exceeding the amounts budgeted for the assignment.

❑ Not every single item has to be accounted for in every communication. For example, if there is a problem in one mechanical area that needs to be brought to the client's attention, it is sufficient to lump together the total amount for design development on one line and focus on the specific production problem. As with any form, avoid compulsively filling out every item regardless of whether it is useful or necessary.

❑ To avoid confusion, cross out or delete items under scope of work which are not applicable to the project.

❑ The term "in-house" refers to the use of the designer's own equipment for production. There are some existing standard prices for this kind of usage. For example, photocopies are routinely billed to clients at an average of

15 cents per copy. Photostats produced by an in-studio camera are often billed to clients at approximately the same rate that it costs to produce them at a commercial stat house. Rather than having to track varying stat-sheet sizes and billing them at different rates per size, an average size can be determined with a fixed cost per sheet for all stats regardless of their size.

❏ Typography generated by designer-owned computers can translate into considerable savings for clients. While savings should be passed along, there are significant costs to owning (or renting/leasing), operating, servicing, and supplying the necessary equipment. One approach is to charge separately for the time that the computer operator spends on generating type with a mark-up on his or her hourly rate to include the expenses of the equipment. Another approach is to calculate the total cost of the equipment, including finance payments, servicing, and supplies, and divide the total sum by the approximate volume of use for the same period of time used to calculate the cost of the equipment. The result is a per-page charge. A mark-up should always be included in these calculations to account for internal administrative time and a profit. It is not unreasonable to make considerable profits on in-house equipment when there is still savings being passed along to the client. Such material would otherwise have to be purchased and marked-up, resulting in a much higher cost to the client.

❑ **Estimate Form for Client**   ❑ **Preliminary Budget and Schedule**   ❑ **Budget and Schedule Review**

Client _____   Date _____

Project _____   Project No. _____

SCOPE OF WORK	TIME			MONEY		
	Allocated	Used	Balance	Budget	Spent	Balance
Design Development _____						
Client Meeting						
Concept Planning						
Preliminary Sketches						
Copywriting						
Art Direction						
Illustration						
Photography						
Comprehensive Layouts						
Changes						
Subtotal						
Mechanical Production _____						
Typography						
Typography (in-house)						
Hand Lettering						
Graphs and Charts						
Technical Renderings						
Photoprocesses						
Line Art						
Photoprints						
Color Stats						
Color Keys						
Retouching						
Photostats (in-house)						
Photocopying						
Other						
Proofreading						
Finished Mechanical Boards						
Changes						
Separations						
Bluelines						
Corrections						
Printing						
Printing Supervision						
Fabrication						
Installation						
Subtotal						
Miscellaneous _____						
Research Materials						
Stylist						
Models						
Travel						
Local Messengers						
Courier Services						
Toll Calls and Fax						
Subtotal						
Total						

This is **not** a contract. The information provided is solely for estimating purposes. Fees, expenses, and time schedules are minimum expected amounts only.

By _____

Proposal Form

In assigning new work, one of the most significant factors in the client's selection process is the designer's proposal. Reputation, recommendations, astute marketing, and self-promotion all play an important part in capturing a client's attention, but among the final deciding elements in winning the assignment is a well-organized, clearly written, concise, and reasonable proposal.

Proposals are often used by clients to compare fees of several designers being considered for an assignment. A ballpark proposal basically needs to let the client know how much would be charged for the prospective work. Such proposals winnow out which designers are to be seriously considered, at which point a more extensive proposal is usually requested. While ballpark proposals need not be extensive, they should include a brief description of the assignment, fee amounts, and expense policy. Schedules and specific terms need not be itemized, but it should be stated that this is a preliminary proposal and that, if accepted, additional items such as a schedule of payment and terms will be forthcoming.

In a competitive situation price is not always the sole determining factor in assigning work. It is more significant to be within the range of given price quotes than to be dramatically lower or higher. An extreme departure from the general range of price quotes signals a lack of understanding of the assignment, desperation, or indifference. If information provided by the client is vague or incomplete, it is especially necessary to include a brief phrase indicating that the proposal is predicated on available information and that any additions or changes will have an impact on the final cost of the project. For example, inexperienced clients tend not to understand how many sketches they are entitled to for a basic fee. For nonvisual or new clients, it is useful to specify the number of sketches that are to be provided, followed by a price quote for additional sketches should they be necessary.

The most important pieces of information that need to be conveyed are (1) an understanding of the assignment by means of a brief description; (2) methodology, or an outline of the working process; (3) fees and expense policy (billables, schedule of payment, mark-ups, etc.); (4) time schedule, if possible; and (5) basic terms (copyright, credit, changes, termination, etc.). While not every proposal needs to include all of these points, the more informative the proposal, the stronger its impact. Proposals can be standardized, such as the example included here, or they may be written in composition style; they should not be longer than two to three pages.

Some designers construct their proposals so that if they are accepted the client merely needs to return a signed copy and the proposal then becomes a letter of agreement. In such instances, it is very important to include a specific list of terms governing the assignment. Items such as the number of sketches, billing for extras and changes, transfer of rights, credit, sales tax, liability, and termination fees all have to be addressed. However, for a straight proposal most designers limit the terms to a few basic essentials on the premise that too many unfavorable terms for a client will automatically put the designer out of the running. At the very least, it is important to mention the number of sketches that will be provided for the stated fee, cost of additionals if necessary, and information about termination. Should the proposal be accepted, a more detailed list of terms may be worked out in a final letter of agreement or contract, such as the Project Confirmation Form that appears in this book.

Filling in the Form

Give the name and address of the client, the date, project title, and contact person in the design office. Describe the scope of the work in the areas indicated. Specify which expenses are reimbursable by the client and the amount of the markup. List those expenses that will be billed at cost. Indicate creative services that will be needed, such as photography or illustration, and also the costs, mark-ups, and totals for production expenses. Specify the schedule of payments and the termination policy. If the form is to serve as a contract, the client's representative should also sign and date the form. On the back of the form indicate the number of sketches in Paragraph 1 and the cost for additional sketches. Fill in the hourly cost for revisions in Paragraph 2. Reserve appropriate usage rights in Paragraph 3. Specify how long the client has to pay in Paragraph 5. Provide a credit line in Paragraph 6. State the length of the work in Paragraph 7.

Using the Form

❏ Include a brief description of the project. (Project Description)

❏ The cost for all phases of the work should be itemized and broken down by time and expense (Scope of the Work). Some categories that might be listed in this itemization include: research, sketches, design development (layout, art direction), mechanicals, and press/ fabrication supervision.

❏ List the number of preliminary sketches to be included in quoted fee and state the cost for each sketch in excess of that number. (Paragraph 1)

❏ State what the fee will be for client revisions to finished, camera-ready mechanicals. (Paragraph 2)

❏ List any rights of usage of mechanicals that the designer will retain. (Paragraph 3)

❏ State the number of days that the client has in which to complete payment. (Paragraph 5)

❏ Specify how the designer's credit line should appear on all printed material. (Paragraph 6)

❏ Allow for additional fees for overtime and rush jobs. (Paragraph 7)

❏ Tell the client that any quotes are estimates based on information attained through the client. Should the client revise the scope or type of work required the quote will also be subject to revision. (Paragraph 8)

❏ State that to complete work in a timely manner, client must provide all pertinent information at reasonable intervals. (Paragraph 10)

❏ The designer should either close the form with his or her signature, or include a cover letter with the proposal.

❏ Review the negotiation checklist for the Project Confirmation Form, which might be used to reach final agreement if the Proposal Form is not signed by the client. Note the different statement of some points in the Project Confirmation Form and consider incorporating additional provisions into the terms of the Proposal Form.

Checklist for How to Write Composition Style Proposals

❏ In an introductory paragraph itemize what is to be designed and, if appropriate, mention the source of information about the project. This description need not include all technical specifications, but should include the type of product (logo, brochure, packaging, etc.), size, number of colors and pages, and other descriptive characteristics.

❏ Under the heading of "scope of work" list the phases of the project's development, such as sketches, design development, layouts, mechanicals, and printing supervision. If the prospective client is not familiar with the design process, it is helpful to list phase by phase what the designer will do and at what points the client will be presented with material.

❑ For "time schedule" give, if possible, an estimate of the length of time each stage will take. State clearly that this estimate is predicated on the client's timely provision of information and approvals at each stage.

❑ For "fees and expense policy" either provide an overall flat fee to cover the assignment and then break that number down into a series of payments; or provide a fee amount for each phase of the job's development and let that be the basis for the payment schedule. Indicate any additional costs that may not be included in the fee, such as reimbursable expenses, author's alterations, and other client-directed changes.

❑ The expenses of photography, illustration, copywriting, printing, and fabrication are also generally not included in the designer's fee and should be specified as such. Offer estimates of approximate costs, if possible, and indicate mark-ups wherever they apply.

❑ Termination fees must be specified as a standard part of every agreement. Termination (also known as "kill fee") refers to the discontinuation of an assignment by either the client or the designer. Some designers require advance payment for each stage of work to be started and specify that this amount is the kill fee in the event the assignment is stopped at any time during this stage of work. With this kind of a schedule of payment the designer is always financially at an advantage and need not resort to withholding work if payments are behind schedule.

❑ Another way of organizing all of this information is to include fees and time schedules along with the descriptions for each separate stage of work. In this format, there should be a separate paragraph for the payment schedule and another for information about reimbursable expenses.

Proposal Form

Client_____   Date_____

Project_____   By _____

Project Description _____

_____

_____

_____

_____

Scope of Work	Schedule	Fees
1. Concept Planning_____	_____	_____
_____	_____	_____
_____	_____	_____
_____	_____	_____
2. Design Development_____	_____	_____
_____	_____	_____
_____	_____	_____
_____	_____	_____
3. Mechanical Production_____	_____	_____
_____	_____	_____
_____	_____	_____
_____	_____	_____

Expenses Policy	Schedule of Payment

Reimbursables with _____% markup: _____

_____

_____

Reimbursables at cost: Termination Fee: _____

All information in this proposal is subject to the terms printed on reverse side.

If these terms and rates meet with your approval and we may begin work, please sign below and return a copy to this office.

_____   Date_____
Company Name

_____
Authorized Signature

Terms

1. Fee quoted includes _____ preliminary sketches; additional sketches are $_____each.

2. Fee quoted includes one set of finished camera-ready mechanicals; changes necessitated by client revisions and/or additions following approvals at each stage (sketches, layout, comps, mechanicals), other than for Designer's error, are billed additionally at $_____ per hour.

3. Rights: All rights to the use of the mechanical boards transfer to the Client, except as noted: _____.

4. Ownership of mechanical boards transfers to client upon full payment of all fees and costs.

5. All invoices are net due within _____ days.

6. Credit: Unless otherwise agreed, Designer shall be accorded a credit line on all printed material, to read as follows:_____

7. Fees quoted are based on work performed during the course of regular working hours (based on a _____ hour week). Overtime, rush, holiday, and weekend work necessitated by Client's directive is billed in addition to the fees quoted.

8. All fees and costs are estimated. Changes in scope of work and/or project specifications require a revision of the information provided on reverse.

9. The information contained in this proposal is valid for thirty days. Proposals approved and signed by the Client are binding upon the Designer and Client commencing on the date of the Client's signature.

10. The Designer's ability to meet deadlines is predicated upon the Client's provision of all necessary information and approvals in a timely manner.

Credit Reference Form

New and unknown clients are naturally a welcome challenge to every design firm. They may bring stimulating problems with opportunities for interesting design solutions. They may develop into long-term artistically and financially rewarding relationships. They may also bring financial havoc. Whether a client is simply new or entirely unknown, a serious look at the newcomer's financial history would be a prudent first step toward deciding whether or not to spend the time and effort needed to produce an excellent proposal.

In the case of a new but not unknown client, a call or two to the vendors or individuals known to have business relationships with the client might produce the necessary information.

In the case of an entirely unknown prospective client, the only way to obtain financial information is to ask the prospect for a list of credit references. Designers are often reluctant to go to this extent to protect their interests; however, they should remember that they have to furnish the same information to obtain credit with vendors and suppliers. Large or small typesetters, stat houses, and equipment suppliers, among others, rarely open accounts with designers without first verifying their credit worthiness.

It is not enough simply to ask the client to fill out this form. It is up to the designer to actually contact the references and ask about the prospect's credit status. Some credit agencies may require a fee for this service. Generally, neither banks nor individuals will commit to stating the exact dollar worth of the prospect (which in any case is not the issue). However, they are able to provide information about the prospect's cycle of payments and general financial history. Be prompt in starting your credit inquiries, since the references may take some time to respond or require a written request. At the same time the client may want to move ahead.

In the event the prospective client is unable to furnish any credit history and the designer still chooses to take the assignment, the only recourse in protecting the designer is to require that the client pay at least one-third to one-half of the fee in advance, with the balance due prior to the delivery of mechanicals; reimbursables should be billed with regular frequency (weekly or bimonthly), and payments should be received within a specified number of days. It is also advisable to make arrangements for large out-of-pocket expenses to be billed directly to the client or estimated in advance and paid at least partially in advance.

Filling in the Form

Fill in the name of the company, its address, telephone number, and the name of the contact at the company who is the liaison on the account. Fill in the date. The client fills in the names, addresses, telephone numbers, account numbers and/or contact names of those references he or she prefers to list. An authorized representative of the client signs and dates the form on the bottom, below the statement granting the designer permission to run a credit check. The "notes" column is reserved for the designer to jot down information as it is relayed through phone conversations. If responses are in written form, positive or negative responses can be indicated in the "notes" column and a copy of the letter attached to this form.

Using the Form

The most important questions to ask when checking the prospect's credit are:

❑ How long has the reference done business with the prospect?

❑ What type of business relationship has the reference had with the prospect?

❑ Has the reference ever extended credit to the prospect?

❑ If credit has been extended, what is the maximum amount of this credit?

❑ How many days does the prospect take to pay its bills?

❑ Does the prospect pay all invoices in full as presented, or does it pay on account (in small but regular payments over a drawn out period of time)?

❑ Ask if the reference would have any reservation about extending credit to the prospect in the amount of the likely billing.

Credit Reference Form

Company Name_____   Date_____

Address_____   Telephone_____

_____   Contact_____

Lenth of time in business:_____

Credit Agencies (Name & Address)	Telephone No.	Account No.	Notes
1			
2			
3			

Banks (Name & Address)	Telephone No.	Account No.	Notes
1			
2			
3			

Trade (Name & Address)	Telephone No.	Contact
1		
2		
3		

Personal (Name & Address)	Telephone No.	Notes
1		
2		
3		

By the signature below, authorization and permission is granted to contact the references listed above for the purpose of verifying available credit information on the company and/or individual named above.

_____   By:_____   Date_____
Company Name   Athorized Signatory

This form (and a number of others) are reduced for ease of reference.
They appear full-size on the 8 1/2 X 11" pages in the tear-out section.

Jobs Master Index

What is the start up procedure for any new job?

Immediately after an agreement has been reached (presumably in writing) between the client and designer concerning scope of work, fees, and terms, the designer can consider the job in-house and begin work. At this point, a few simple procedures will effectively organize any job and allow the tracking of its financial and scheduling history.

The first step in opening a studio job is to assign it the job number which will be used to identify every aspect and component of the assignment. The job number is also referred to as the project number, particularly in client communications. *The Jobs Master Index is the source of all job numbers.* It is a chronological list of every job, past and present, in the studio and is the simplest and clearest way of knowing what jobs are in-house, who is doing them, how long they have been going on, and whether or not they have been billed.

The "job number" list can begin with any number initially, but then must follow consecutively thereafter. Job numbers may be keyed to the year, such as "91-102," but regardless of how the numerical order is determined, it is best to keep it uncomplicated and as brief as possible since it will have many applications. Always keep the numbers in sequence. Do not fill in the numbers in advance since some assignments may need additional space. For jobs with several distinct subparts which need to be tracked separately for billing purposes, use one job number for the overall name of the assignment/client and use subnumbers or letters to indicate the different parts of the job (also keep separate job sheets for such subnumbers or letters). See example A.

If jobs are unrelated, but have the same client and came in-house at the same time, use separate job numbers. See example B.

Filling in the Form

In the "date" column fill in the date the job is officially assigned to the studio. Under "client" fill in the company name of the client. Under "job name" indicate briefly what the assignment is, for example: "Toy catalogue—Spring"; "Sinatra Album—front & back"; or "The Joy of Baking—recipe cards."

Example A

Date	Client	Job Name	Designer	Invoice #	Job #
5/17/91	Aztec House	Restaurant —logo	GL		2201-A
"	" "	—menus	DF		2201-B
"	" "	—signage	JK		2201-C
"	" "	—ads	GL		2201-D

Example B

Date	Client	Job Name	Designer	Invoice #	Job #
6/30/91	Atlantis Magazine	Supplement—Oct.	SZ		2219
"	" "	Arts Section—Nov.	GL		2220
"	" "	Cover Illus—Dec.	JB		2221

Under "designer" fill in the initials of the designer who will have primary responsibility for the assignment. In the "invoice number" column enter the invoice number(s) on the day or days the job is billed. Then fill in the job number.

Using the Form

❑ Use job numbers on job sheets, time sheets, purchase orders, billable invoices, and for logging stat, Xerox, blueprint, color key, and other in-house charges. The job number is the link to all job-related costs and materials.

❑ Post the jobs master sheet near the copier and stat machines, messenger desk, and long-distance log books so that employees can easily refer to it and use job numbers consistently. It greatly simplifies record-keeping.

❑ Open a job bag for each new job. Red manilla, kraft, string-tie envelopes (approximately 22-by-28 inches), are useful for keeping all job related materials in one place. Affix a label to the envelope showing the job number, client and job names, and the date the job was opened.

❑ Open a job file to store copies of agreements, work orders, receipts, and back-up copies of billable invoices. It is useful to clip all correspondence and nonbillable papers to the inside of the front cover of the file folder (chronological order, most recent on top). Since designers are frequently required to show back-up for reimbursable expenses such as typography, photoprocesses, printing, messengers, travel, and so on, the file folder is a convenient place to gather back-up copies of these billables.

❑ As soon as a bill has been posted to the appropriate job sheet, pull one of the copies of the bill (if it comes in duplicate), or make an extra copy of bills that don't, and place the copy in this job file. When it is time to bill out the job, all of the necessary back-up copies will be in this file—along with all of the correspondence relating to the assignment. When the job is completed and billed, simply file the folder in either chronological, alphabetical, or subject order for future reference. Quite often it is helpful to be able to check back to earlier proposals and contracts when estimating or negotiating new jobs.

Jobs Master Index

Date	Client	Job Name	Designer	Invoice #	Job #

Job Sheet

Cost accounting, or keeping track of time and costs expended on a project, is essential to maintaining a regular and accurate billing system. The job sheet is the detailed record of all time and costs incurred during the course of an assignment. It is useful to record time and costs regardless of any fee arrangement since even miscellaneous unbillable time and expenses have an impact on profits when all real costs are fully known. Items such as special supplies, research time, and very long and frequent client meetings not originally calculated into the fee may significantly diminish what might have seemed to be an acceptably profitable job. The advantage of knowing all costs, including extras, is the possibility of more astutely negotiating time and fees of prospective assignments, or perhaps renegotiating a current one.

Job sheets can be used to analyze the following information:

Time spent doing the job. This category can be further notated to indicate specific aspects or phases of jobs. For example, in a packaging assignment with several components, it may be necessary or useful to know how much time was spent on design development, comping, and mechanicals, or how much time it took to do various individual packages.

Billable costs. Graphic designers can expect to bill and often mark up the cost of typography, photoprocesses, retouching, and other outside production services. Special supplies, prototypes, couriers, even postage and toll calls may be billable depending upon the arrangement with the client. All of these items and their mark-up rate are to be negotiated before the deal is finalized. Indicate with an "NB" to the right of the "total" column those items which are nonbillable.

Profitability. In some instances a designer may be working for an hourly fee, in which case accurate records are indispensable. However, when on a flat fee basis, it is still essential to be able to determine whether the fee was adequate for the time spent doing the work. To examine profitability, subtract total actual costs from the total amount billed for the job (not including the tax), for example:

Flat Fee minus Nonreimbursable Project Costs = Gross Profit

$700.00   minus $200.00   = $500.00

Gross Profit   minus   Overhead Allocation   =   Net Profit

$500.00   minus $300.00   = $200.00

Overhead refers to the general cost of running the design studio. These include the costs of rent, insurance, utilities, cleaning, maintenance, general supplies, and so on. None of these items are billable to specific assignments, but, along with salaries and profit, they must be figured into the fee structure of every assignment. The overhead factor must also be calculated into the hourly rates used when billing is based on time rather than on a flat fee. To calculate overhead expenses, add up all of the monthly business costs (which are not billable as reimbursable expenses) and divide this total figure by the number of jobs in the studio per month; the resulting number is the dollar amount which every job has to produce to cover the minimum cost of running the business.

For example:

Rent	$ 400
Equipment & Supplies	$ 200
Utilities	$ 100
Insurance	$ 75
Accounting & Legal	$ 30
Promotion	$ 100
Salary	$3,000
Total	$3,905

This designer must produce $3,905 worth of gross profit every month, just to stay in business. If this designer averages six assignments per month, approximately $650 of every assignment goes directly to paying for overhead. Naturally, higher-paying jobs cover the lower-paying ones, but somehow the final numbers have to average the basic minimum amount needed to cover the essential expenses of the business. To calculate the minimum hourly rate needed to cover overhead expenses, divide the monthly overhead costs by the number of working hours in the month, for example:

$$\$3905 \div 160 = \$24.41$$

$24.41 is the minimum hourly rate the designer can charge in order to meet his or her monthly expenses, including his or her salary. If there are other salaries in the business which are not billable to jobs, these salaries must also be considered as part of the overhead. Remember, however, that this calculation assumes all project costs are reimbursable and does not account for profit.

Calculating profit into fees and hourly rates is not an exact science. Generally, designers add an additional 20 percent to 100 percent into the overhead figure, for example:

$24.41 (minimum hourly rate)
x .20 (percent profit desired)
_____
$ 4.88 + $24.41 = $29.29 (total hourly rate)

Naturally, any hourly rate has to have a reasonable relation to what other professionals are charging for similar work and what the market will bear—that is, how strongly the client wants to work with the designer. Flexibility is important in determining fees and hourly rates.

Filling in the Form (Page One, Side One)

Enter the job name. Use the same name as the one used on the jobs master index. Fill in the full corporate name of the client. Fill in the complete address, telephone number, and name of the contact (including title and department). If the party to be billed is different from the client, fill in the "bill to" category.

Indicate if shipping is to client or designer; fill in if different from either. If the client issues a purchase order specifying the terms and costs of the agreement, keep a copy of it in the job file and fill in the purchase order number. Fill in the dates the job came in house, when sketches are due, the finish due date, when the mechanicals are accepted, and any other important date next to "other."

Fill in the overall fee amount. Check the "time" box if billing is based on time. Specify if production, or other time is billable. Also indicate the markup factor, if any. Check the "costs" box if out-of-pocket expenses are billable, and, if applicable, the mark-up factor. Check the "tax" box if sales tax will need to be collected and fill in the appropriate rate.

In the columns for "inv #," "date," and "amt" fill in the invoice number, the date of the invoice, and its total amount every time a bill is sent to the client for this assignment. Some jobs may require only one invoice, other jobs may need to be billed in stages and will make use of the additional columns provided.

Fill in the space left for "job number" in large or bold numbers so that it will be easy to read when flipping through these sheets.

In the area under "costs" list one by one all of the items related to this job, whether billable or not. This process is called "posting" and should take place regularly and frequently, or at least once a week.

In the "date" column fill in the date the cost is being entered (or the "posting" date). Under "item" fill in the name of the vendor, or the person whose time is being entered. For "description" of a vendor's bill, fill in the vendor's invoice number and the date of the invoice. For "description" of a person's time, fill in the date of the person's bill for services, or for employees, the time period during which these hours were accrued. It is also helpful to jot down the stage of work these hours covered, such as "sketches," "research," "mechanicals," etc. In-house costs such as photocopying, stats, and color keys should be tallied and entered weekly or bimonthly, with the date of the tally under "description." The "hours/rate" column is for both outside labor and in-house employees. "Rate" information should be actual, not marked-up since this worksheet reflects only actual costs. For "total" fill in the total amount of the item entered.

Using the Form

❏ Start a job sheet as soon as a number has been assigned to the job from the jobs master index which is best located in the front of the job sheet book and thus also serves as its index. Both these forms work best in loose-leaf style three-ring binder books.

❏ Posting should take place when time sheets have been collected for payroll and when job-related bills are being paid.

❏ Indicating job numbers on time sheets and payable invoices makes it easier to post these items to individual job sheets.

❏ In-house services such as photocopying, stats, color keys, and other production items should have tally sheets near the respective equipment, along with a copy of the jobs master index for easy reference.

❏ When an assignment is ready for billing, tally all related items separately. For example, add up typography, photoprocesses, photocopying, stats, and so on, separately. Add up each individual's time and/or total cost separately. For billing, show each separate cost item by item. Factor in markups after each item has been totalled.

For example:

Typography

$47.89
35.67
12.00
98.04
—————
$193.60 x 20% = 38.72 (markup)

$193.60
38.72
—————
$232.32 (total cost of typography including markup to client)

John Designer (Free-lance)

10 hours
7 hours
4 hours
11 hours
—————
32 hours

32 hours x $20 (hourly rate) = $640 (cost to studio)

$20 x 2.5 (markup factor) = $50/hour

$50 x 32 (hours) = $1,600 (cost to client)

Filling in the Form (Page One, Reverse Side)

The "Summary of Costs" is a comprehensive way to itemize the estimated and actual job costs, markup factors (if applicable), and the total amount of each item billed. Use this summary when calculating the total costs and billing for an assignment. Interim summaries are useful if there is a specific budget for reimbursables; if interim summaries are needed, do them in pencil and the final tallies in ink.

"Description of Job" should be a brief and precise summary of what the client is expecting to receive. "From" refers to the source of the information given, such as, "phone/A.Jones/5-17-90", or "P.0. #4558/5-19-91", "meeting w/A.Jones/ 6-20-91", and so on.

"Bidding Estimates" is a handy space to list any production quotes requested by the client. For example, the client may require two to three printing estimates; another client may request a couple of bids on typography, and so on. "Date" refers to when the bid was received from the vendor (the same date presumably that this is being filled in); "item" is the type of service being quoted; "vendor" is the name of the supplier providing the bid; for "amount" fill in the actual amount, not including any markups; "quoted to" refers to the person to whom this information is being transmitted; under "accepted" place a check mark next to the accepted bid.

Any time a client makes changes in the scope of work which was the original basis of the job, note under "work order changes" the date of the change, revision, extension, or whatever new item is being requested; under "item" list or describe the specific request made by the client; under "given by" write in the name of the person authorizing the change.

Using the Form

❏ The reverse side of page one of the Job Sheet is intended to serve as a quick reference where all the pertinent details of the assignment are in summary form. The paperwork backing up all of this information should be located in the job file. These summaries relate to the following forms which can be found in this book: "Description of Job" relates to the Proposal Form; Letter of Agreement and the Contract Form.

"Bidding Estimates" relate to the Estimate Form for Suppliers (Estimate Request)

"Work Change Orders" relate to the Work Change Order Form

Job Sheet (Supplementary Pages)

Uncomplicated short term assignments will generally need only one page of the job sheet. However, when assignments are complex and involve a greater variety and frequency of services, or continue for long periods of time, the supplementary forms can be added on to accommodate the listing of on-going time and costs.

Follow the same procedure for filling in these forms as described under Filling in the Form, Page One, Side One.

For jobs which require periodic billing for fees and costs, draw a heavy line or skip a space under the last item included in each separate invoice and jot down the invoice number by this line so that it will be easy to see where to start tallying for the next invoice.

Job Sheet (Page One Side One)

INFORMATION

Job_____

Client_____

Address_____

_____

Contact_____

Telephone_____

Bill To_____

_____

Ship To_____

_____

P.O. #_____

DATES

Job In_____   Sketch Due_____

Finish Due_____   Other_____   Accepted_____

BILLING

Fee_____   ❑ Time   ❑ Costs   State Tax_____%

Inv #_____   _____   _____
Date_____   _____   _____
Amt_____   _____   _____

Inv #_____   _____   _____
Date_____   _____   _____
Amt_____   _____   _____

Job Number [   ]

COSTS				
Date	Item	Description	Hrs/Rate	Total
___	___	___	___	___
___	___	___	___	___
___	___	___	___	___
___	___	___	___	___
___	___	___	___	___
___	___	___	___	___
___	___	___	___	___
___	___	___	___	___
___	___	___	___	___
___	___	___	___	___
___	___	___	___	___
___	___	___	___	___
___	___	___	___	___
___	___	___	___	___
___	___	___	___	___
___	___	___	___	___
___	___	___	___	___
___	___	___	___	___
___	___	___	___	___
___	___	___	___	___
___	___	___	___	___
___	___	___	___	___
___	___	___	___	___
___	___	___	___	___
___	___	___	___	___
___	___	___	___	___
___	___	___	___	___
___	___	___	___	___
___	___	___	___	___
___	___	___	___	___
___	___	___	___	___

Job Sheet (Page One Reverse Side)

SUMMARY OF COSTS

Item	Est	Actual	M/U	Billed
Fee				
Meetings				
Design Development				
Comps				
Mechanicals				
AA's				
Extras				
Art Direction				
Printing Supervision				
Travel				
Typography				
Line Art (Stats)				
Photo Prints				
Retouching				
In-House Stats				
In-House Photocopies				
Illustration				
Photography				
Stylist				
Other Talent				
Printing				
Fabrication				
Local Messengers				
Courier Services				
Toll Calls & Fax				
Tax				
Totals				
Profit				

DESCRIPTION OF JOB

Source_____

BIDDING ESTIMATES

Date	Item	Vendor	Amt	Accepted

WORK CHANGE ORDERS

Date	Item	Ordered By

Job Sheet (Page Two)

COSTS

Date	Item	Description	Hrs/Rate	Total

COSTS

Date	Item	Description	Hrs/Rate	Total

Time Sheet

Regardless of whether assignments are billed on a flat fee or hourly rate basis, it is essential to know exactly how much time is spent by all staff members on every assignment; additionally, it is useful to know how nonbillable time is being used. Naturally, it is important to have an accurate record for jobs billed by the hour, mostly to ensure that all billable time is reimbursed, and partly in the event the client requests an audit of time-keeping records. While it is not customary to attach staff members' time sheets to client invoices, many formal assignment agreements contain language entitling the client to review the designer's records pertaining to the client's specific assignment.

Time should also be accounted for on projects that are billed on a flat fee basis. Working backwards, the fee itself is generally based on an approximation of the amount of time to be spent on the project, with a mark up to include profit and overhead expenses (nonbillable costs such as rent, utilities, insurances, etc., are discussed under the Job Sheet section). To approximate the time to be spent, the designer needs to think the assignment through its technical stages...how many pages...how many colors...how big...how complex...will there need to be outside services such as illustration and photo retouching?...does the client have a tendency toward conducting numerous and lengthy meetings?... etc. Naturally, there are other factors in determining prices, such as the intrinsic value of the finished piece (usually keyed to its uses, volume of reproduction, and breadth of its distribution), the market for which it is being produced, as well as the size and financial resources of the client; all of these factors are more or less fixed and known in the earliest stages of the project. Time is the variable in determining fees and the most important key to profitability on a flat-fee-based assignment. The more exact the understanding is of the technical production and client contact required, the more accurate the estimation of the time required. As a safety device, some designers customarily add 15 percent to whatever number of hours they estimate will be needed to complete the assignment.

Filling in the Form

Every time sheet must have the name of the person whose time is being recorded. The total period of time being recorded is filled in next to "dates"; also include the month and year. Fill in the "job number" column so that whoever is posting time sheets to job sheets does not have to refer to the jobs master index every time a job name appears.

Fill in the job name, including the client name, for example:

> Acme—brochure
> Eccentrix—album logo.

Indicate the aspect of the job that was worked on under "job phase," for example:

> Cover
> Interior layout
> Presentation meeting

Specify the particular activity performed under "activity," for example:

> Research—picture files
> Comps
> Mechanicals—revise pages 2 and 3
> Press supervision

Indicate the number of hours worked on each job, phase, and activity separately for each day. Fill in the number of hours which were overtime under "OT." Check the box under "OK to bill" if appropriate. Whoever is responsible for posting time to job sheets checks the box under "posted" as each line is transferred to the appropriate job sheet. Any time spent on nonbillable activities should also be noted and specified as indicated. Holidays and sick days should also be listed.

Using the Form

❑ Everyone who is required to fill out a time sheet—and for the sake of billing, principals and other senior personnel are also accountable—should fill out their time sheet daily, since it is often hard to remember exactly how much time is spent on specific activities when

the studio is busy and people are rushing to get work out.

❑ Time sheets should be checked and initialled by job captains or senior designers, as appropriate. Principals and senior staff usually turn their time sheets directly over to whomever is posting.

❑ Time sheets should be posted weekly so that no more than a few days are needed to prepare billing when an assignment is complete or ready for the next phase of billing.

Time Sheet

Name_____ Month_____
Dates_____ Year_____

Job#	Job Name	Job Phase	Activity	Mon Reg/ OT	Tue Reg/ OT	Wed Reg/OT	Thu Reg/OT	Fri Reg/ OT	Total Reg/ OT	Ok to Bill	Posted

Nonbillables

Administration							
Clean-up							
Promotion							
Holidays							
Sick Days							
Other (explain)							
Totals							

Approved_____

Studio Production Schedule

It is characteristic of the graphic design profession that work must be produced on deadline schedules. One of the designer's most serious concerns is the ability to complete assignments on time. In order to calculate the blocks of time needed to meet deadlines, the designer should work out a studio production schedule after receiving the details of a new assignment. Most commonly, designers calculate production schedules by working backward from the final due date for delivering the assignment. This form is a simplified version of the very detailed Preliminary Budget and Schedule which appears in this book.

Filling in the Form

Fill in all the known due dates. Block out the amount of time, using specific dates, needed to complete each activity listed. Estimate the dates when specifications, copy, approvals, and other material will be needed from the client. Let the client know that the designer's ability to meet deadlines is predicated upon the client providing the necessary information, material, and approvals on time. Under "to/from" indicate, unless self-explanatory, in which direction material is moving, or more specifically, the names of vendors or free-lancers who are responsible for providing material. Fill in the actual date items are completed and delivered.

Using the Form

❑ Designers may choose to attach a copy of the studio production schedule to the agreement or contract for the assignment in order to assure that the necessary information and approvals from the client are delivered on time, thus enabling the designer to meet his or her deadlines. In the event the client is negligent in providing necessary material, a record of the actual dates of such deliveries may help substantiate the designer's problems with delivering the job on time.

❑ A production schedule is good for planning later stages of jobs where the designer is dependent upon others for completing the assignment. There are several benefits to contacting prospective illustrators and photographers in the planning stages of a project: it gives the designer time to review the necessary portfolios; the prospective talent has an opportunity to come in on the conceptual stage and may possibly contribute additional insight or useful suggestions; and, finally, the selected talent is able to allocate the appropriate time necessary to produce the work. Printers also appreciate being able to schedule print runs in advance and may be more cooperative in finding the exact papers or other materials specified.

Studio Production Schedule

Client_____   Job Number_____

Job Name_____   Date_____

Item	Dates	Due Dates	To/From	Delivered
Preliminary Meetings				
Materials Due (Specs/Copy)				
Sketch Presentation				
Client Approval				
Design Development				
Layouts/Comps				
Client Approval				
Art Direction				
Photography				
Illustration				
Other (Copywriting)				
Type Specifications				
Mechanicals				
Client Approval				
Revisions/Corrections				
Separations				
Printing				
Fabrication/Installation				
Delivery				

Project Status Report

Designers use project status reports for long term and complicated projects, where they are invaluable in keeping clients informed. The report includes information about what is presently going on, who is waiting for what, from whom, and when. Used regularly, these reports help smooth communications between designer and client and may also be helpful in keeping subcontractors tuned into the rhythm and direction of the project. For short term, less complex assignments, project status reports can be used to prod a client out of a stalled situation. This report can also be particularly useful to nonvisual or inexperienced clients because it gives them a clear picture of what is expected to happen and in what order. Using standard professional terminology (such as comps, mechanicals, proofs, bluelines, and so on) also allows the client to become familiar with the language as well as the process of graphic design. Finally, a status report helps to identify those individuals who have responsibility to carry out specific tasks. It is a clear, but nonaggressive way of getting people to respond to specific issues and needs.

Filling in the Form

Fill in the name of the person(s) who will be receiving this report, or the corporate name of the client if it is to be circulated widely. Fill in the name of the project; list the names of additional people who will be receiving a copy of this report; the job number; and the date of the report. (This format may also be used for summarizing the minutes of meetings, in which case the date of the meeting should be indicated as well.)

There are two ways to use this form: (1) For short specific tasks that correspond to the list of phases, check mark the applicable phases, and fill in the items and other information in the spaces provided; (2) if the need is to discuss one or two topics in greater length and detail, check the phase appropriate to the discussion and use the entire space available on the sheet to outline the points to be made.

Using the Form

❑ Someone on the design team should take notes during client meetings. These may simply be key phrases informally jotted down, or they may be standard, outline-style notes. Whatever the form, the ability to articulate the client's needs and ideas briefly, along with a written record of critical decisions, serves as a great advantage in conceptualizing and moving a project along.

❑ When it is useful to keep subcontractors (such as free-lance artists, vendors, and manufacturers) appraised of project developments, this form can be addressed either directly to them, or they can be included in the general distribution of copies. Very often, subcontractors are either directly affected by specific changes on a project or they simply need to know whether the work is proceeding according to schedule.

❑ Most assignments have critical deadlines and it is important for everyone involved to know how their contribution fits into the overall scheme. It cannot be overstated that clear, timely, and accurate communications are essential to the success of group projects.

Project Status Report

To_____   Project Number_____   Date_____

Copies_____   Project Title _____

Phase	Item	Status	Next Action	Date Due
Preliminaries				
Design Development				
Art Direction				
Layouts				
Mechanicals				
Printing/Fabrication				
Other				

Work Change Order Form

In the course of virtually any kind of assignment, it is almost inevitable that clients will request some kind of changes. Whether changes are required in the conceptual stage, during design development, layout, or even during the printing or fabrication process, it is very useful to document these changes. First, to verify the exact nature of the change, and second, to justify any additional billing that the extra work necessitates. Typesetters refer to such changes as "author's alterations" (also known as AA's) and always bill such changes as extras.

A brief and simple form is easier for clients to read, sign, and return than addenda to contracts, or even letters outlining the new client instructions. While it is desirable to have clients return these forms signed and dated to indicate approval, when they do not, the language printed on the bottom of this form is intended to protect the designer from an unresponsive client.

Filling in the Form

Fill in all the information concerning client name, project name, project number (same as job number), and the date. Indicate the stage of work during which this particular change is being requested. Specify under "content" and/or "specifications" which aspect of the work is being changed. Under "remarks," state briefly what the work change is. If lengthy copy changes have been required, attach a copy of such changes to this sheet. Indicate the estimated additional time and/or cost it will take to make these changes. Specify the number of days during which the client may correct the form. If possible, have the form signed by the client and returned.

Using the Form

❑ Keep track of all additional time and costs incurred by changes in the project's scope or specifications. If the client questions additional charges, these work change orders serve as proof that additional work took place either at the client's behest or with the client's approval for changes initiated by the designer.

❑ Keep this form in the job file. Jot down a brief summary of work change orders on the project's job sheet, page one, reverse side.

Work Change Order

Client _____   Date_____

Project_____   Project No._____

Work Change Requested By_____

Stage of work

Sketches	_____
Comps	_____
Layout	_____
Mechanicals	_____
Bluelines	_____
Printing/Fabrication	_____
Typesetting	_____
Art Direction	_____
Other (explain)	_____

Content Change

Conceptual	_____
Copy	_____
Illustration	_____
Photography	_____

Specifications Change

Typography	_____
Colors	_____
Size	_____
Pagination	_____
Reproduction	_____
Shipping	_____
Other (explain)	_____

Remarks_____

_____

_____

_____

_____

This is not an invoice. Revised specifications on work in progress represents information that is different from what the designer based the original project proposal. The following estimated charges in time and cost are approximate.

Estimated Additional Time_____

Estimated Additional Cost_____

Kindly sign and return a copy of this form. The information contained in this work change order is assumed to be correct and acceptable to the client unless the designer is otherwise notified in writing within_____ days of the date of this document.

Approved by_____   Date_____

Estimate Request Form

Whenever clients and designers prefer to have a variety of choices in the selection of outside services (such as typography, photoprocesses, illustration/photography, fabrication, and so on), it becomes necessary to request bids from eligible and appropriate suppliers. To avoid confusion in evaluating these bids, it is useful to provide the competing suppliers with exactly the same description of the work to be performed. This form may also be used to back up a verbal quote when the supplier has been selected without preliminary bidding. Although it is clearly a quotation of approximate fees and costs, the estimate request helps to control significant variations in vendor billings.

Filling in the Form

Fill in the name of the client and project, the date, the project (job) number, the name of the person requesting the estimate, and his or her telephone number. Fill in the name, address, and telephone number of the vendor/supplier in the space marked "to." Fill in the delivery date. Fill in "specifications/description" in as great a detail as possible; include as much information as necessary to accurately estimate the work to be done. Leave blank the spaces for estimate, sub-total, tax, shipping/delivery, total, and deposit required. The vendor/supplier should sign the estimate next to "quotation by" and fill in the date.

Using the Form

❑ When requesting bids, fill in the heading and the specifications/description part of the form; make as many copies as needed to distribute to the prospective bidders (plus one for the designer's files); and then fill in the "to" section with the name of each individual bidder on each separate copy of the form. This way it is certain that everyone has exactly the same instructions on which to base their bids.

❑ If necessary, send a copy of all estimate requests to the client. Include information which will have an effect on the bid, even though it is not exactly related to the job; for example, if there are complicated shipping requirements, or if the assignment will require the vendor to travel, or any other service that will be in addition to the basic required work.

❑ Keep this form in the job file. Jot down a brief summary of bidding estimates on the project's job sheet, page one, reverse side.

Estimate Request Form

Client_____   Date_____

Project_____   Project No._____

Request By_____   Telephone_____

To_____

_____

_____

SPECIFICATIONS/DESCRIPTION		
Quantity	**Item**	**Estimate**
_____	_____	_____
_____	_____	_____
_____	_____	_____
_____	_____	_____
_____	_____	_____
_____	_____	_____
_____	_____	_____
_____	_____	_____
_____	_____	_____
_____	_____	_____
_____	_____	_____
_____	_____	_____
_____	_____	_____

Delivery Date_____   Subtotal _____

                                              Tax _____

SPECIAL NOTES   Shipping/Delivery _____

_____   Total_____

_____

_____   Deposit Required_____

_____

Quotation by_____   Date_____

This is not a purchase order. The information contained in this form is to provide a basis for estimating the cost of the services requested. It is understood that the estimated costs are approximate and that final billing will be adjusted according to specific instructions provided in a purchase order or contract.

Kindly fill in the information requested in the shaded area under Estimate, sign, date, and return a copy of this form by _____ Thank you.

Purchase Order

The purchase order serves as a written notice to vendors, manufacturers, and other suppliers, including free-lance artists, to begin work on a specific assignment or to deliver goods. Many vendors will not proceed without a written purchase order. For the design studio, the purchase order form is handy in two ways. First, it is a record of when goods are ordered, from whom, and when they are expected to be delivered. Second, when invoices are being checked, purchase orders are useful for verifying precisely what was ordered. In the event the supplier is in error, the purchase order serves as verification of the original order. Additionally, if prices are included on the purchase order form, the designer is quickly able to justify and post the invoice incurred by the order.

As with job numbers and invoice numbers, purchase orders start with any number and then continue in chronological order. It is very helpful, but not absolutely necessary, to have forms with preprinted numbers. It is, however, essential to make the forms either in duplicate or triplicate. Pressure sensitive paper, carbons, or photocopying will serve this purpose. At the very least, the designer will need to send the original copy to the vendor and keep a copy for him or herself. Studios with separate bookkeeping departments would need a third copy for the bookkeeper's records.

Filling in the Form

Write in the number of the purchase order, date of the order, the client and project names, and the project number (job number). In the space under "to" fill in the name of the vendor, the address if it is a new or unknown supplier, and the name of the contact or sales representative at the vendor's place of business. In the space for "schedule" fill in the date the job must be received in the designer's hands and check the appropriate level of urgency. In the space under "specifica-

tions" fill in the instructions for the work to be done or the goods to be delivered. Give quantities, sizes, dimensions, and any other specific information necessary to communicate exactly what is expected. If using a catalogue to order from, give item numbers, catalogue page numbers, descriptions, and so on. Be absolutely precise. In the space for "shipping address" fill in the name and address of where the goods are to be delivered. The designer should compute the subtotal and total, if costs are known in advance. In the space for "bill to" fill in the name and address of where the supplier is to send his or her invoice if other than the designer. Print or clearly sign the order and fill in the telephone and extension number where the designer can be reached for questions.

Using the Form

❑ Purchase order forms should be on letterhead or some other form of stationery that clearly shows the name of the designer, the name of the firm, its address and telephone number.

❑ Remember that both rush and overtime will incur additional costs. It is best to check what these will be in advance. Markups for rush and overtime orders can be as much as 100 percent and more. Overtime refers to work that must be completed overnight, on weekends, or on holidays.

❑ Provide a sketch, if necessary, to convey a full understanding of the order. The more detailed and descriptive an order, the less chance there is of having to accept and pay for mistakes.

❑ Most suppliers prefer to bill the designer directly and usually are not pleased to have to bill a third party. This is a detail that should be worked out in advance. The supplier may require a deposit, as well as bank and business references before acceding this point.

❑ Copies of completed purchase order forms should be kept all together in one place, such as a loose-leaf ring binder, in numerical order (most recent number used on top); or, in the job file together with all the other paperwork for the project.

❑ If the designer chooses to use purchase order forms to contract free-lance work, he or she must remember to include information pertaining to copyright, usage, and credit lines that the free-lance artist may require. Also, it is useful to require the free-lancer's social security number so that Form 1099 can be completed (as required by the Internal Revenue Service for any payments of $600 or more to independent contractors).

❑ Be certain that the rights which the designer obtains from free-lance artists or photographers are at least as great as the rights which the designer must transfer to the client.

❑ If the designer must oversee and pay for the printing, consider using the Contract with Printer form that appears in this book. It seeks to protect the designer from the many problems that may arise, including the issue of client satisfaction with the printed piece.

Purchase Order

Number [   ]

Client_____   Date_____

Project_____   Project No._____

To_____

_____

_____

Schedule: Date Required _____   ❏ Regular   ❏ Rush   ❏ O.T.

Specifications: _____
_____
_____
_____
_____
_____
_____
_____
_____
_____
_____
_____
_____

Ship to_____   Subtotal _____

_____   Tax _____

_____   Shipping _____

_____   Total [_____]

Bill to_____

_____

_____

_____

Ordered by_____   Tel._____ Ext._____

Requisition Form

Small design studios rarely make use of internal requisition forms. Larger studios tend to have more of a need for them since there is greater efficiency in ordering supplies and distributing them from a central source. Further efficiency is achieved by not duplicating orders, being able to take advantage of discounts on larger orders, and minimizing loss and disappearance of supplies. This form is flexible in that it acknowledges different types of supply orders according to their source. These forms can either be distributed to all staff members, or they can be held by one person in each department.

Filling in the Form

The person who is requesting supplies fills in his or her name, telephone extension number, and the date of the order. Using the "source codes" indicated on the form, identify each item by the appropriate code and give the information requested for that code number. Check mark whether the items are needed urgently or within the regular time frame for such orders. Provide job numbers wherever applicable.

Using the Form

❑ For billable items, the job number is immediately applied to purchase orders as well as to order forms, thereby simplifying the task of posting when the invoice for the order arrives.

❑ It is helpful to have an up-to-date selection of art and office supply catalogues that are easily accessible to anyone wishing to place an order.

Requisition Form

Name_____

Telephone Extension _____ Date _____

Delivery
❑ Regular
❑ Rush

Source Codes

1. Catalogue (Include name of catalogue, page number, item number, brief description, quantities, and unit prices)

2. Internal Supplies (Include name of item, description including sizes and colors, and quantities)

3. Other (Include name of source, address and telephone number, a description of the item including sizes, colors, quantities, and unit price)

Source Code	Description	Unit Price	Job Number

Payables Index

The payables index is used to track incoming invoices, whether or not they are related to billable jobs. It is handy for checking monthly statements and determining whether or not bills have been approved. It also contains all of the necessary information to relocate lost bills. Incoming invoices should be gathered on a daily or biweekly basis (depending upon the volume of payable bills). After recording the required information to the payables index, distribute the bills to those who will be approving them. (A closed-sided manilla file folder with each person's name on the tab is handy for this purpose.)

Filling in the Form

Under "date received" fill in the date the bill came into the studio. Under "company/OL name" write in the name of the company or individual printed on the bill (free-lancers are called "outside labor" in bookkeeping circles). Indicate the total amount of the bill under "amount." Write in the invoice number and the date of the invoice. "Att" refers to the person in the studio who is responsible for approving this particular bill. When the invoice is returned, write the date it was returned in the "approved" column. Job-related bills are now ready for posting to job sheets, after which they can be paid and filed; bills not related to jobs can be paid and filed directly.

Using the Form

❏ Every bill for expenses incurred by any specific job, or the studio in general, should be looked over by the art director, designer, or other individual who ordered the corresponding material or services. (Generally, job captains on large assignments have the responsibility of reviewing such invoices.)

Any person responsible for reviewing invoices should indicate the following on each invoice:

❏ If the invoice is related to a job, indicate the job number even if it is not a billable expense, but incurred by the needs of the project. Indicate with an "NB" those job-related bills that are not billable to the client.

❏ If the bill is for a studio expense and not related to any specific job, simply indicate "studio" on the bill.

❏ The person approving the bill should place their initials on it.

❏ Indicate the date the bill is approved.

❏ If the bill is for more than one job, divide the sum appropriately and indicate the amounts applicable to the separate jobs.

❏ If the bill is incorrect, this is the time to make adjustments with the vendor. Ask the vendor to reissue a correct bill, if possible, rather than making the corrections by hand.

❏ File a copy of all billable invoices in file folders identified on the outside by individual job numbers. Every job should have this "back up" file to collect copies of all reimbursable expenses (which are then sent to the client when the job is billed to substantiate these expenses). This file can be the same as the one described in the Job Sheet section of this book.

Payables Index

Date Received	Company/OL Name	Amount	Invoice #	Date	Attention	Approved

Transmittal Form

The transmittal form is most frequently used as a cover letter for enclosures, attachments, and any other kind of material being disseminated within or outside of the studio. The advantage of having one multi-use transmittal form is that it eliminates the need to create individually written letters every time material needs to be circulated. Also, the information on the form is comprehensive, thereby uniformly communicating the necessary facts about the accompanying material. If possible, have the form printed on the designer's letterhead; if that is not feasible, make sure the firm's name, address, telephone, and fax numbers are clearly readable.

Filling in the Form

Fill in the name of the recipient, his or her company name, the job number if applicable, the name of the person sending the material and the names of additional people who will also be receiving a copy of this form. Next to "for" check the reason for sending the enclosed or accompanying material. Next to "via" check the means by which this communication is being sent. For "enclosed" check mark the nature of the attachment or enclosure. For "disposition" indicate whether the material is to be returned, kept, or distributed. Use the space left for "remarks" for additional messages.

Using the Form

❑ Under remarks state that ownership of the artwork and all rights are reserved to the artist, unless otherwise specified.

❑ Keep copies of all transmittals in the job file.

❑ If the transmittal is not job-related, keep copies in either a file or a loose-leaf, ring-bound notebook with the most recent date in front.

❑ If material of great value is being transmitted (such as original photographic transparencies), obtain adequate insurance to cover loss and damage.

❑ If the material transmitted is valuable, indicate who is responsible for loss or damage–including during shipment.

Transmittal Form

To_____ From_____

Company_____ Date_____

Project_____ Project Number_____

Copies to_____

For

❑ Review   ❑ Files   ❑ Information
❑ Approval   ❑ Distribution   ❑ As Requested

Via

❑ Fax (Number of pages, including transmittal_____)
❑ Messenger   ❑ UPS   ❑ Inter-Office
❑ Courier Service (_____)
❑ US Mail (regular)   ❑ US Mail (express)
❑ Freight Forwarder (_____)

Enclosed

❑ Artwork   ❑ Comps   ❑ Mechanicals
❑ Photographs   ❑ Color Xeroxes   ❑ Transparencies
❑ Blueprints   ❑ Sepias   ❑ Mylars
❑ Typeset Copy   ❑ Samples   ❑ Model
❑ Article   ❑ Book   ❑ Promotion Package
❑ Other (_____)

Disposition

❑ Kindly Reply   ❑ Return   ❑ Keep   ❑ Distribute

Remarks_____
_____
_____
_____
_____
_____
_____
_____
_____
_____
_____
_____

All artwork remains the property of the artist with all rights reserved, unless specified otherwise in writing.

Artwork Log

This form is used to track the whereabouts of artwork sent out by the studio. Artwork includes original art, sketches, mechanicals, transparencies, prototypes, models, and so on. The form is also intended to serve as a permanent record of the location of artwork stored within the studio. It is not uncommon for designers to be responsible for the storage of mechanical boards, particularly for corporate identity and other projects involving stationery, in which case it is important to be able to locate materials quickly when they are needed for reorders and changes.

Filling in the Form

Fill in the date and time the artwork is being sent; the job number to which it relates, the name and address of its destination, and a very brief description (such as "original art," "sketches," "me-chanicals," "models," etc.). For "via" indicate how the work is being sent (for example, UPS, messenger, name of courier service). If applicable, indicate the date the work is due back in the studio. When the work is returned, note the date and where it is to be found the next time it is needed ("location").

Using the Form

❏ This form either can be located in or near the studio's traffic area and filled in by individual staff members; or, it can be the responsibility of one person in the studio—perhaps the receptionist— in which case all staff members need to remember to transmit the necessary information to this person. In large firms, individual departments maintain their own log files.

Artwork Log

Date	Time	Job #	To	Description	Via	Due Back	Returned	Location

Billing Index

The billing index is the list of all monies billed to clients for on-going or completed work. One of the most critical pieces of information for any business is the amount and schedule of expected income.

While bookkeepers and accountants are familiar with "accounts receivables" and keep a separate ledger of all outgoing invoices, it is helpful on the studio level to be able to quickly and easily check when jobs have been billed, whether or not they have been paid, and how long bills have been outstanding (not paid).

The billing index is also the source of all invoice numbers. Invoice numbers are to billing what job numbers are to cost accounting. An invoice number is an identifying "tag" that serves to keep track of invoices within both the designer's and the client's bookkeeping systems. When assigning invoice numbers, begin with any number and then follow consecutively thereafter. It is best not to link invoice numbers to job numbers or purchase order numbers. An uncomplicated, independent, sequential list of numbers is less likely to create confusion for both manual and computerized billing systems. To allow for varying space needs, do not fill in the numbers in advance.

Filling in the Form

Fill in the date that will appear on the invoice under "date." Fill in the invoice number and the job number relating to the assignment being billed. For "billed to" fill in the name of the client as it appears on the jobs master index. With two to three words identify the job, or use the job name as it appears on the jobs master index. Fill in the fee, total production costs and tax, if applicable, in the designated columns. Under "amount due" fill in the total amount of the invoice. The "paid" column is filled in with the date and the check number when the payment is received.

Using the Form

❑ The billing index is used for invoicing regular fees and costs on studio jobs, consulting fees, re-use fees for reproduction rights to artwork, and any other kind of item for which the studio should be paid or reimbursed.

❑ Use this index concurrently in preparing invoices. First, determine the fee or rates due, tally up all the billables from the job sheet and assign a number to the invoice from the billing index. Write up the invoice and fill in the rest of the information indicated on the billing index.

Billing Index

Date	Invoice #	Job #	Billed To	Job Name	Fee	Production	Tax	Total	Paid

Invoice Forms

Billing is the financial pipeline of the graphic design studio. Considering that the turnaround time for payment can be anywhere from thirty to ninety days and more, it is imperative that billing be done quickly and regularly. Whenever possible, establish a payment schedule even for small assignments. At the least, arrange for an advance payment against the total fee with the balance and reimbursable expenses to be due upon completion of the work. If the job is based on one-time payment, it should be billed as quickly as possible.

Two different sample invoice forms are reprinted here. Although the information contained in each is nearly identical, the second is more detailed than the first, and is intended as a preprinted, two-sided form. The first form (Form 17) would probably be most appropriate for a beginning design firm that might not generate enough volume to require preprinted forms. This basic invoice format fits easily on most letterheads. Pressure sensitive pullouts, carbons, or photocopies can provide the necessary duplicates. Once the studio has a steady volume of billing, it is more convenient to have preprinted forms, especially if they are printed in multiple copies on pressure sensitive paper. It is not advisable to have preprinted forms numbered in advance. Forms of any kind are generally more useful when they allow for flexibility, especially in the numbering process. The billing index is the running log and source of all invoice numbers.

Filling in Form 17

Fill in the date of the invoice, its number (from the billing index), and the project number (same as the job number). Fill in the full corporate name of the client and its address. "Att" may be either the contact on the assignment, the name of the client's purchasing agent, or simply "accounts payable." If a purchase order has been issued by the client, fill in that number. State the name of the assignment next to "project title."

The easiest way to write the "description of services" for an invoice is to copy or summarize with a list in the same language used in the assignment's proposal, letter of agreement, or contract. If the agreement contains a schedule of payment, the invoice can be a direct copy of that schedule. If there is an overall flat fee, list the services performed by the studio, but do not assign dollar amounts to each service, just summarize the list with an all encompassing phrase, such as, "Design and Production Fee." The rest of the invoice is actually a summary of all the billables listed on the job sheet for the assignment. If the time spent by individual staff members is separate from the overall fee arrangement, a simple statement may suffice.

For example:

Staff Time..$____

Some clients may require a more detailed accounting, such as:

Staff Design Time (1/5/90-2/7/90)...............$____

Or:

Staff Design Time (1/5/90-2/7/90; 287 hrs) $____

Or:

John Designer
(1/5/90-2/7/90) 121 hrs @ $___/hr...............$____

Jane Designer
(1/5/90-I/9/90) 27 hrs @ $___/hr...............$____

Al Mechanical
(1/5/90-2/7/90) 139 hrs @ $___/hr...............$____

It is best to check in advance what the client's preference is in notating this kind of information.

A separate list of reimbursable expenses follows the description and fees section. Subtotal all the items, indicate if the invoice is subject to tax, show the amount, and fill in the total for the entire bill. In the "terms" section fill in the number of days in which the studio expects to receive payment from the client.

Indicate the disposition of the original artwork and the expected time frame of its return. Indicate the specific rights which the client is entitled to. For example: "Product packaging"; "First time reproduction in North America, hard cover version"; "Television advertising"; "All rights, except for television advertising."

Filling in Form 18

Fill in the date of the invoice, its number (from the Billing Index) and the project number (same as job number). Fill in the full corporate name of the client and its address. "Att" may be either the contact on the assignment, the name of the client's purchasing agent, or simply "accounts payable." If a purchase order has been issued by the client for the assignment, fill in that number. State the name of the assignment next to "project title."

Under "design development" check mark the specific services covered by the fee. In the space underneath, either leave blank except to fill in the fee amount in the space next to "design s/t" or list any items which carry a separate fee amount, for example:

Design	$2,500
Mechanicals	$2,500
Illustration	$4,000

Place the total design development amount in the space next to "design s/t."

For "mechanical production and reimbursable expenses" check all of the applicable items, indicate either hourly rates, cost-per-item, or markups under "rate" and the total amount of the individual item. The space underneath is for any necessary additional information. Fill in the "production s/t," a subtotal of the design and production figures, the applicable tax, if any, and the grand total. On the reverse side of the form, fill in the information needed to complete the "terms" section.

Using the Form

❑ One of the inevitable snags in producing bills quickly is that suppliers and free-lancers often do not submit their bills in time to be approved and posted to the job sheet. This results in incomplete back-up information. First, it is necessary to urge all outside providers to be timely in their billing, and second, it may be necessary to bill a job in stages. The studio can issue a bill for the fee or billable time and all available costs with a note on the invoice, clearly written and in an obvious location, saying, "Additional production costs to follow." When all such costs have been received, approved, and posted, a second invoice can follow, notated under "description":

Additional production costs, as per our invoice #_____, date _____.

❑ When markups are arranged in advance, the hourly rates shown on the invoice should automatically reflect the marked-up rate. Some studios prefer to standardize hourly rates by having tiers of different rates for different types and levels of work. For example:

Senior Design Staff	$_____	per hour
Regular Design Staff	$_____	per hour
Mechanical Art Staff	$_____	per hour

While this system is easier to compute and notate, it should be carefully evaluated so that the resulting dollar amounts actually cover the full cost of each individual within his or her tier.

❑ If markups are specified for production expenses in the assignment agreement, the invoice should automatically reflect the marked-up rate. It is not necessary to itemize every markup computation; it is recommended, however, that the back up material for each separate item be stapled together with an adding machine tape showing both the tally of the attached bills, and the markup computation. This is a courtesy to the client's bookkeeper, and it is also helpful in moving invoices along.

Invoice

Date _____

Invoice Number _____

Project Number _____

To _____

_____

_____

_____

Attention _____   Purchase Order No. _____

Project Title _____

Description of Services	Fees/Costs
_____	_____
_____	_____
_____	_____
_____	_____
_____	_____
_____	_____
_____	_____
_____	_____
_____	_____
_____	_____
_____	_____

Subtotal _____

Tax _____

Total _____

Terms: Kindly remit amount due net _____ days.

All original artwork remains the property of the artist, except as noted: _____
_____

Rights transferred are limited to: _____

❏ All other rights reserved.

❏ Rights specified herein and ownership of mechanical boards transfer to client upon full payment of all fees and costs.

Invoice

Date _____

Invoice Number _____

Project Number _____

To _____

_____

_____

_____

Attention _____   Purchase Order No. _____

Project Title _____

Design Development

❑ Client Meetings   ❑ Copywriting   ❑ Photography

❑ Concept Planning   ❑ Art Direction   ❑ Illustration

❑ Preliminary Sketches   ❑ Comprehensive Layouts   ❑ Changes

_____

_____

_____

_____

Design Subtotal _____

Mechanical Production and Reimbursable Expenses

	Rate	Total		Rate	Total
Type Specifications			Proofreading		
Typography (out)			Finished Mechanicals		
Typography (in)			Changes		
AA's			Separations		
Hand Lettering			Printing		
Graphs and Charts			Printing Supervision		
Technical Rendering			Fabrication		
Line Art			Installation		
Photoprints			Research Materials		
Color stats			Stylist		
Color Keys			Models		
Photoprocessing			Travel		
Retouching			Local Messengers		
Stats (out)			Courier Services		
Stats (in)			Freight		
Photocopying			Toll Calls & Fax		
Other _____			Production Subtotal (2) _____		
Production Subtotal (1) _____			Subtotal _____		
			Tax _____		
			Total _____		

See reverse side for terms of agreement.

Terms

Kindly remit amount due net _____days.

All original artwork remains the property of the artist, except as noted:

_____
_____
_____
_____

Rights transferred are limited to:

_____
_____
_____
_____

❏ All other rights reserved.

Credit line to read as follows:

_____
_____
_____

Rights specified herein and ownership of mechanical boards transfer to client upon full payment of all fees and costs.

Monthly Billing Statements and Collection Letters

Designers may request that clients pay invoices within any reasonable number of days, but in reality it is more likely that clients will pay according to their own payment cycles. However, once payment for an invoice is overdue, (anywhere from ten to sixty days, depending on the specific time frame established within the proposal or agreement for the assignment), the designer has two options. He or she can call the client contact, mention the possibility of an oversight, and ask the contact to look into the matter. Or, the designer can send the client a billing statement such as Form 19. Such statements are routinely sent by all vendors and creditors and are merely a summary of the amounts due for payment.

In the unfortunate event that there is no response to the first statement or call, another call can be placed to the client contact or the client's bookkeeper. If this does not yield satisfaction within a very short time, a second notice such as Form 20 should be sent. For a usually reliable client, it can be a copy of the first statement with a stamped or hand written note saying "Second Notice." For a new or unknown client, a lack of response to the statement may necessitate one more contact before sending a final notice.

A final notice, such as Form 21, is the last direct communication the designer sends to the client. The letter should be sent in a way that the client has to sign a receipt acknowledging its delivery: messenger, telegram, registered mail, UPS or some other courier service would all serve this purpose.

Filling in the Forms

Fill in the date; the corporate name of the client; its address; and the name of the contact on the assignment or the head of accounts payable next to "att." If the problem concerns one specific assignment, next to "reference" fill in the name of the project, its job number, and the client's purchase order number, if any. If several assignments are involved, state the overall name of the account, if any. List the unpaid invoices. Fill in the name and phone number of the party whom the client should contact and have that person sign the form.

Using the Forms

❑ There is no guaranteed way of avoiding the problem of collecting payment. It is helpful to have all the financial details of an assignment arranged in advance and in writing. Ideally, a copy should be returned to the designer with the client's signature. It is also important to bill promptly and regularly.

❑ Establishing advance payments and a schedule of payments is also extremely useful. It is better to spot financial problems while the designer still has some leverage (such as possession of the mechanicals).

❑ The last recourse is to turn the account over for collection either by a reputable agency or attorney. This may involve paying 25 to 40 percent of the money collected as a collection fee. Keep in mind that collection agencies can only ask for money. They are not licensed to practice law and cannot bring lawsuits. If the client is unlikely to pay, retaining an attorney for an hourly fee might be the best approach.

❑ For amounts of less than a few thousand dollars, depending upon locale, small claims court may be a viable option. Local court offices provide information about filing claims.

❑ Tenacity is important to the success of collecting, but in some cases it may be necessary to be flexible in accepting partial payment with a revised payment schedule.

Statement

Date _____

To_____

_____

_____

_____

Attention_____

Reference_____

_____

_____

Please be advised that payment for the following has not been received as of today's date.

Date of Invoice	Invoice Number	Amount Due
_____	_____	_____
_____	_____	_____
_____	_____	_____
_____	_____	_____
_____	_____	_____
_____	_____	_____
_____	_____	_____
_____	_____	_____
_____	_____	_____
_____	_____	_____

We would greatly appreciate your prompt attention and earliest payment possible. Please call if you have any questions or comments about this statement.

Call_____ Telephone Number_____

Signature_____

Second Notice

Date _____

To_____

_____

_____

_____

Attention _____

Reference_____

_____

_____

Statement Date	Date of Invoice	Invoice Number	Amount Due
_____	_____	_____	_____
_____	_____	_____	_____
_____	_____	_____	_____
_____	_____	_____	_____

Sorry not to have heard from you. This is the second time we have had to contact you about this overdue account.

If you cannot make immediate payment in the full amount, please call right away.

Call_____   Telephone Number_____

Signature_____

Final Notice

Date _____

To_____

_____

_____

_____

Attention_____

Reference_____

_____

_____

This account is now seriously in arrears. We have repeatedly requested payment and have neither received payment nor have we been contacted with an explanation.

We must collect immediately, and, if we are not satisfied within ten days, we have no choice but to turn this account over for collection. Be aware that this process may result in additional legal and court costs to you and may damage your credit rating.

It is not too late to contact us.

Call_____   Telephone Number_____

Signature_____

Project Confirmation Agreement

The project confirmation form serves as a contract to be used when the client is ready to move forward on a project based on a proposal or estimate. While the client can make a contract simply by signing a proposal, such as Form 2 in this book, the project confirmation form offers a more detailed and formal understanding between the parties.

Ideally, the client will review a proposal and request whatever changes are necessary. Then the designer will fill in the project confirmation form to conform to what the parties have agreed and both parties will sign to make a binding contract. By signing such a form before the commencement of an assignment, the parties resolve many of the issues likely to cause disputes. Since the goal with any client is to create a long-term relationship, the avoidance of needless disputes is a very positive step.

Filling in the Form

Fill in the date and the names and addresses for the client and the designer. In Paragraph 1 describe the project in detail, attaching an additional sheet to the form if needed. Specify the number of sketches and designs, any other specifications, the form in which the job will be delivered if not as mechanicals, any other services to be rendered by the designer, the client's purchase order number, and the designer's job number. In Paragraph 2, fill in how many days it will take to go from starting work to sketches and from approval of sketches to finished designs. In Paragraph 3 give the limitations on the rights granted and specify whether the client's rights are exclusive or nonexclusive. In Paragraph 5 state the fee. In Paragraph 7 fill in the markup for expenses and the amount of any advance to be paid against expenses. In Paragraph 8 give a monthly interest rate for late payments. Fill in Paragraph 9 if advances on the fee are to be paid. Check the boxes in Paragraphs 11 and 12 to indicate whether

copyright notice or authorship credit will be given in the name of the designer. State in Paragraph 13 the percentages of the total fee that will be paid for cancellation at various stages of work. In Paragraph 14 fill in a value for the original design and any other originals, such as illustrations or photographs. In Paragraph 16 specify who will arbitrate disputes, where this will be done, and give the maximum amount which can be sued for in small claims court. In Paragraph 17 give the state whose laws will govern the contract. Both parties should then sign the contract.

Negotiation Checklist

❑ Describe the assignment in as much detail as possible, attaching another sheet to the contract if necessary (in which case the project description would refer to the attached sheet). (Paragraph 1)

❑ Give a due date for sketches, which can be expressed as a number of days after the client's approval to start work. (Paragraph 2)

❑ If the client is to provide reference materials, the due date should be expressed as a number of days after the designer's receipt of these materials. (Paragraph 2)

❑ The due date for delivery of mechanicals can be expressed as a number of days after the client's approval of sketches. (Paragraph 2)

❑ Time should not be of the essence.

❑ State that illness or other delays beyond the control of the designer will extend the due date, but only up to a limited number of days.

❑ State that the grant of rights takes place when the designer is paid in full. (Paragraph 3)

❏ Limit the grant of rights to the final form of the designs, so rights in sketches or other work products are not transferred. (Paragraph 3)

❏ Specify whether the client's usage rights will be exclusive or nonexclusive. (Paragraph 3)

❏ Limit the exclusivity to the particular use the client will make of the designs, such as for product packaging, a point of purchase ad, a direct mail brochure, and so on. This lets the designer benefit from other future uses which the client might make of the designs.

❏ Name the product or publication for which the designs are being prepared. (Paragraph 3)

❏ State the language of permitted usage.

❏ Give a geographic limitation, such as local, regional, the United States, North America, and so on. (Paragraph 3)

❏ Limit the time period of use. (Paragraph 3)

❏ Other limitations might include the number of uses, the number of printings (or quantity printed), and the size of the work when reproduced. The concept behind such limitations is that fees are based in part on usage.

❏ For contributions to magazines, such as when the designer might do an illustration, the sale of first North American serial rights is common. This gives the magazine the right to be the first magazine to make a one-time use of the illustration in North America. This could be limited to first United States serial rights. If no agreement about rights is made for a magazine contribution, the copyright law provides that the magazine has a nonexclusive right to use the illustration as many times as it wishes in issues of the magazine but can make no other uses.

❏ All rights not granted to the client should be reserved to the designer, including rights in sketches and any other preliminary materials. (Paragraph 4)

❏ If the client insists on all rights or work for hire, offer instead a provision stating, "Designer shall not permit any uses of the Designs which compete with or impair the use of the Designs by the Client." If necessary to reassure the client, this might also state, "The Designer shall submit any proposed uses to the Client for approval, which shall not be unreasonably withheld."

❏ In the face of a demand for all rights or work for hire, advise the client that fees are based in part on rights of usage. The fee for all rights or work for hire should be substantially higher than for limited usage.

❏ If the work is highly specific to one client, selling all rights for a higher fee would be more acceptable than for a work likely to have resale value for the designer.

❏ If the client demands a "buyout," find out how the client defines this. It can mean the purchase of all rights in the copyright; it may be work for hire; and it may or may not involve purchasing the physical design as well as the copyright.

❏ Do not allow the client to transfer or assign usage rights without the consent of the designer, since the client may benefit from re-use fees that more appropriately belong to the designer.

❏ The fee must be specified. For a lengthy or complex project, a schedule of fees coordinated to stages of completion might be attached to the form . (Paragraph 5)

❏ The obligation of the client to pay sales tax should be included. Many states charge sales tax if a physical object (such as a mechanical board) is sold to or altered by the client. This is in contrast to sales of reproduction rights which are often not subject to sales tax. The laws vary widely from state to state. The designer must check the law in his or her state, since the failure to collect and pay sales tax can result in substantial liability. (Paragraph 5)

❏ If additional usage rights are sought by the client, additional fees should be agreed upon and paid. (Paragraph 6)

❏ If it is likely a certain type of additional usage will be made, the amount of the re-use fee can be specified. Or the re-use fee can be expressed as a percentage of the original fee.

❏ The client's obligation to reimburse expenses to the designer should be specified to avoid misunderstandings. (Paragraph 7)

❏ If expenses will be marked up, this should be stated. The rationale for marking up expenses is the use of the designer's funds until reimbursement and the extra paperwork. If expenses are modest, however, some designers prefer to cover them in the fee. (Paragraph 7)

❏ If expenses will be significant, provide for an advance against expenses. (Paragraph 7)

❏ Specify that any advance against expenses is nonrefundable unless, of course, the expenses are not incurred. (Paragraph 7)

❏ For substantial expenses, such as printing, illustration, or photography, consider whether the client should contract and pay directly for such expenses. If the client does contract directly, can the designer still justify a markup in view of the designer's supervision of the supplier?

❏ If the client insists on a binding budget for expenses, provide for some flexibility, such as a 10 percent variance, or for the client to approve items which exceed the variance.

❏ Require payment within thirty days of delivery of the finished art. (Paragraph 8)

❏ State that interest will be charged for late payments, but be certain the interest rate is not usurious. (Paragraph 8)

❏ Deal with the issue of payment for work-in-progress which is postponed but not cancelled. A pro rata billing might be appropriate. (Paragraph 8)

❏ Specify advances to be paid against the fee, either on signing the contract, on approval of sketches, or at both times. A schedule of payments is especially important for an extensive job. (Paragraph 9)

❏ State that any advances against the fee are nonrefundable. This is not done in Paragraph 9 because of the interplay with the cancellation provision in Paragraph 13.

❏ Revisions can be a problem. Certainly the designer should be given the first opportunity to make revisions. (Paragraph 10)

❏ If revisions are the fault of the designer, no additional fee should be charged. However, if the client changes the nature of the assignment, additional fees must be charged for revisions. (Paragraph 10)

❏ Consider limiting the amount of time the designer must spend on revisions, whether or not the revisions are the fault of the designer.

❏ If the client ultimately has revisions done by someone else, the designer should reserve the right to have his or her name removed from the designs. (Paragraph 10)

❏ With respect to revisions or the assignment itself, additional charges might be specified for work which must be rushed and requires unusual hours or other stresses.

❏ Any revisions or changes in the assignment should be documented in writing, if possible, since there may later be a question as to whether the changes were approved and whether they came within the initial description of the project. This can be done by using the Work Change Order Form. (Paragraphs 10 and 17; see Form 10)

❏ State whether copyright notice will appear in the designer's name. (Paragraph 11)

❏ State whether the designer will receive name credit with the design. (Paragraph 12)

❏ Specify that the type size for authorship credit and the placement of that credit.

❏ If authorship credit should be given but is omitted, require the payment of an additional fee.

❏ Fees for cancellation at different stages of the assignment must be specified. This very much depends on the nature of the project. For example, sketches may take very little time or they may come close to the finished designs. In the event of cancellation, the designer must also be reimbursed for expenses incurred. (Paragraph 13)

❏ State that the designer shall own all rights in the work in the event of cancellation. (Paragraph 13)

❏ Specify a time for payment of cancellation fees, such as within thirty days of the earlier of client's stopping work or the delivery of the finished designs. (Paragraph 13)

❏ Never work on speculation, which is a situation in which no fees will be paid in the event of cancellation or a failure to use the work.

❏ State that the client owns the mechanicals, but that the designer owns any preliminary sketches or materials as well as any original art or photography. (Paragraph 14)

❏ If preliminary sketches are used by the client, a fee should be charged.

❏ If physical art or photography is to be sold, a separate price should be specified.

❏ Require the client to return art or photography within thirty days of use. (Paragraph 14)

❏ Specify a safe method for the return of the art or photography. (Paragraph 14)

❏ Indicate a value for the art or photography, which can serve as a basis for damages if the client does not take reasonable care of it.

❏ Raise the standard of care which the client must give the art or photography, such as making the client strictly liable for loss or damage while in the client's possession or even in transit.

❏ Require the client to insure the art or photography at the value specified for it. Remember that lost art or lost transparencies can result in very large lawsuits and the designer may be found to be liable for the value of what has been lost. The designer should also consider insuring such original work while in the designer's possession.

❏ Try not to give a warranty and indemnity provision, in which the designer states the work is not a copyright infringement and not libelous and agrees to pay for the client's damages and attorney's fees if this is not true.

❏ If the client insists on a warranty and indemnity provision, try to be covered under any publisher's liability insurance policy owned by the client and ask the client to pay the cost of covering the deductible.

❏ Require the client to indemnify the designer to cover a situation in which the client wants certain materials to be included in the designs but does not request that the designer obtain needed copyright permissions or privacy releases or uses the designs in a way that exceeds the uses allowed by the permissions or releases. (Paragraph 15)

❏ Provide for arbitration, except for amounts which can be sued for in small claims court. (Paragraph 16)

❏ Compare the standard provisions in the introductory pages with Paragraph 17.

Project Confirmation Agreement

AGREEMENT as of the _____ day of _____, 19 _____, between _____,
located at _____ (hereinafter referred to as the "Client")
and _____, located at _____
(hereinafter referred to as the "Designer") with respect to the creation of a certain design or designs (hereinafter
referred to as the "Designs").

WHEREAS, Designer is a professional designer of good standing;

WHEREAS, Client wishes the Designer to create certain Designs described more fully herein; and

WHEREAS, Designer wishes to create such Designs;

NOW, THEREFORE, in consideration of the foregoing premises and the mutual covenants hereinafter set forth and
other valuable considerations, the parties hereto agree as follows:

1. **Description.** The Designer agrees to create the Designs in accordance with the following specifications:
   Project description_____
   Number of finished designs_____
   Other specifications_____
   The Designs shall be delivered in the form of one set of finished camera-ready mechanicals, unless specified
   to the contrary here_____
   Other services to be rendered by Designer_____
   _____
   Client purchase order number_____Job number_____

2. **Due Date.** The Designer agrees to deliver sketches within _____ days after the later of the signing of this Agreement or, if the Client is to provide reference, layouts, or specifications, after the Client has provided same to
   the Designer. The Designs shall be delivered _____ days after the approval of sketches by the Client.

3. **Grant of Rights.** Upon receipt of full payment, Designer grants to the Client the following rights in the Designs:
   For use as_____
   For the product or publication named_____
   In the following territory_____
   For the following time period_____
   Other limitations_____
   With respect to the usage shown above, the Client shall have ❑ exclusive ❑ nonexclusive rights.

4. **Reservation of Rights.** All rights not expressly granted hereunder are reserved to the Designer, including but
   not limited to all rights in sketches, comps, or other preliminary materials created by the Designer.

5. **Fee.** Client agrees to pay the following purchase price: $_____ for the usage rights granted. Client agrees to
   pay sales tax, if required.

6. **Additional Usage.** If Client wishes to make any additional uses of the Designs, Client agrees to seek permission from the Designer and make such payments as are agreed to between the parties at that time.

7. **Expenses.** Client agrees to reimburse the Designer for all expenses of production as well as related expenses
   including but not limited to illustration, photography, travel, models, props, messengers, and telephone. These
   expenses shall be marked up _____ percent by the Designer when billed to the Client.
   At the time of signing this Agreement, Client shall pay Designer $_____ as a nonrefundable advance against
   expenses. If the advance exceeds expenses incurred, the credit balance shall be used to reduce the fee payable
   or, if the fee has been fully paid, shall be reimbursed to Client.

8. **Payment.** Client agrees to pay the Designer within thirty days of the date of Designer's billing, which shall be
   dated as of the date of delivery of the Designs. In the event that work is postponed at the request of the Client,
   the Designer shall have the right to bill pro rata for work completed through the date of that request, while reserving all other rights under this Agreement. Overdue payments shall be subject to interest charges of _____
   percent monthly.

9. Advances. At the time of signing this Agreement, Client shall pay Designer ____ percent of the fee as an advance against the total fee. Upon approval of sketches Client shall pay Designer ____ percent of the fee as an advance against the total fee.

10. Revisions. The Designer shall be given the first opportunity to make any revisions requested by the Client. If the revisions are not due to any fault on the part of the Designer, an additional fee shall be charged. If the Designer objects to any revisions to be made by the Client, the Designer shall have the right to have his or her name removed from the published Designs.

11. Copyright Notice. Copyright notice in the name of the Designer ❏ shall ❏ shall not accompany the Designs when reproduced.

12. Authorship Credit. Authorship credit in the name of the Designer ❏ shall ❏ shall not accompany the Designs when reproduced.

13. Cancellation. In the event of cancellation by the Client, the following cancellation payment shall be paid by the Client: **(A)** Cancellation prior to the Designs being turned in: ____ percent of the fee; **(B)** Cancellation due to the Designs being unsatisfactory: ____ percent of fee; and **(C)** Cancellation for any other reason after the Designs are turned in: ____ percent of fee. In the event of cancellation, the Designer shall own all rights in the Designs. The billing upon cancellation shall be payable within thirty days of the Client's notification to stop work or the delivery of the Designs, whichever occurs sooner.

14. Ownership and Return of Designs. Upon Designer's receipt of full payment, the camera-ready mechanicals delivered to the Client shall become the property of the Client. The ownership of original artwork, including but not limited to sketches and any other materials created in the process of making the Designs as well as illustrations or photographic materials such as transparencies, shall remain with the Designer and, if delivered by Designer to Client with the mechanicals, shall be returned to the Designer by bonded messenger, air freight, or registered mail within thirty days of the Client's completing its use of the mechanicals. The parties agree that the value of original design, art, or photography is $_____, and these originals are described as follows

_____

15. Releases. The Client agrees to indemnify and hold harmless the Designer against any and all claims, costs, and expenses, including attorney's fees, due to materials included in the Designs at the request of the Client for which no copyright permission or privacy release was requested or uses which exceed the uses allowed pursuant to a permission or release.

16. Arbitration. All disputes arising under this Agreement shall be submitted to binding arbitration before _____ in the following location _____ and settled in accordance with the rules of the American Arbitration Association. Judgment upon the arbitration award may be entered in any court having jurisdiction thereof. Disputes in which the amount at issue is less than $_____ shall not be subject to this arbitration provision.

17. Miscellany. This Agreement shall be binding upon the parties hereto, their heirs, successors, assigns, and personal representatives. This Agreement constitutes the entire understanding between the parties. Its terms can be modified only by an instrument in writing signed by both parties, except that the Client may authorize expenses or revisions orally. A waiver of a breach of any of the provisions of this Agreement shall not be construed as a continuing waiver of other breaches of the same or other provisions hereof. This Agreement shall be governed by the laws of the State of _____.

IN WITNESS WHEREOF, the parties hereto have signed this Agreement as of the date first set forth above.

Designer_____   Client_____
                   Company Name   Company Name

By_____   By_____
           Authorized Signatory, Title   Authorized Signatory, Title

Contract with Illustrator or Photographer

FORM 23

Many design projects require illustration or photography. These images must satisfy not only the designer, but the client as well. While images occasionally may be obtained from stock libraries, it is more likely that the designer will assign a free-lance illustrator or photographer to create the needed images. To ensure a greater likelihood of satisfaction, the specifications for the images must be as clear and detailed as possible.

Of course, there must be agreement as to the fee and what is purchased for the fee. Most illustrators and photographers seek to sell only limited rights. If greater rights are purchased, they ask for a higher fee. If the designer is sensitive to this, the best approach may be to ask for limited rights. This should avoid paying for usage rights that are never exploited.

On the other hand, the designer must obtain all of the rights which his or her client needs. In the first instance, the designer must consider what rights will be transferred to the client. Rights can be limited in many ways, including the duration of use, geographic area of use, type of product or publication, title of the product or publication, and whether the use is exclusive or nonexclusive.

The designer may find a lesson in the approach of the illustrator or photographer. Design may have reuse value for the client, even in cases when it has no resale value to third parties. For example, a designer might do a logo for the letterhead of a local business. If the business becomes international and the logo receives innumerable other applications, should the designer receive any payment beyond the initial fee? This will depend on the contractual arrangement between the designer and client.

A client may want all rights. This would mean the client could use the work in any conceivable way. However, on questioning the client, it often develops that the client does not need all rights. Rather, the client wants to prevent competitors from using the illustration or photography (and, of course, the design). Another approach would be for the designer to promise by contract that no use will be made of the design in certain markets without first obtaining the written consent of the client. Or to agree that the client has exclusive rights in those markets where the client faces competitors, but that the client will not unreasonably withhold from the designer (or illustrator or photographer) the right to resell the image or design in a noncompetitive way.

In any case, the designer must act as an intermediary — and, perhaps, as a mediator of sorts — between the demands of the client and the desire of the illustrator or photographer to retain rights and earn more money for greater usage.

Expenses can be a significant aspect of the cost of illustration and, especially, photography. The designer has to know the likely range of these expenses, perhaps by setting a maximum budget to be spent. If the designer requires changes, revisions, or reshoots, this will also add to the expense. Here the designer has to be careful not to be caught in a squeeze between a client with a limited budget and an image cost which exceeds that budget because of changes.

In fact, there is a fundamental issue about payment. Fees and expenses for photographers or illustrators can be substantial. Should the designer become liable for such sums at all? This same issue is present in printing contracts. While designers often pay illustrators or photographers, if the costs are very large it may be better to have the client pay directly. The designer will also have to decide whether to charge a markup on illustration or photography, especially if the client does pay the fee directly.

The illustrator or photographer must also work on schedule. Failure to do this should be a reason for the designer to terminate the contract.

A number of professional references will aid the designer in dealing with photographers or illustrators. These include *Pricing and Ethical Guidelines* (Graphic Artists Guild, distributed by North Light Books), *Professional Business Practices in Photography* (American Society of Magazine Photographers, New York, New York), *Selling Your Photography* by Arie Kopelman and Tad Crawford (St. Martin's Press), and *Selling Your Graphic Design and Illustration* by Tad Crawford and Arie Kopelman (St. Martin's Press).

Filling in the Form:

Fill in the date and the names and addresses for the illustrator or photographer and the designer. In Paragraph 1 give the project title and description, a description of the images to be created, specifications for the images, and any other services the illustrator or photographer will perform. In Paragraph 2 specify the amount of time the illustrator or photographer has to complete the assignment, including any procedures to review work in progress. In Paragraph 3 fill in the nature of the use, the name of the product or publication, and any limitations on the geographic extent or duration of the grant of rights. In Paragraph 4 fill in the amount of the fee, including a computation method if the fee is variable. In Paragraph 5 fill in the maximum amount which the illustrator or photographer is allowed to bill for expenses. In Paragraph 7 indicate how revisions or reshoots will be charged for by the illustrator or photographer. In Paragraph 8 indicate whether or not the illustrator or photographer shall receive authorship credit. In Paragraph 10 fill in which party will own the images delivered as well as any preliminary or other materials (such as outtakes). In Paragraph 13 fill in who will arbitrate, the place of arbitration, and the maximum amount which can be sued for in small claims court. State the term in Paragraph 15. In Paragraph 16 specify which state's laws will govern the contract. Both parties should then sign the contract.

Negotiation Checklist

❏ Describe the assignment in whatever detail is required, attaching another sheet to the contract if necessary. It is very important to determine exactly what the illustrator or photographer is agreeing to do, including any services beyond creating the images (such as proofing). (Paragraph 1)

❏ Give specifications in detail, such as black and white or color (and number of colors, if appropriate), number of images, form in which the images are to be delivered, and whatever else is known at the time of signing the agreement. (Paragraph 1)

❏ Approve the work in progress at as many stages as possible. (Paragraph 2)

❏ Give a due date for the work to be completed, as well as due dates for each approval stage. (Paragraph 2)

❏ If the designer is to provide reference materials, the due date can be stated as a number of days after the illustrator or photographer's receipt of these materials. (Paragraph 2)

❏ If even a short delay would cause serious problems, make time of the essence.

❏ State that illness or other delays beyond the control of the illustrator or photographer will extend the due date, but only up to a limited number of days.

❏ Be certain the grant of rights encompasses all the rights needed by the designer and, of course, by the designer's client. (Paragraph 3)

❏ State that the grant of rights extends to the client or, depending on the designer's contract with the client, gives the designer the right to assign rights to the client. (Paragraph 14)

❏ If it is likely a certain type of additional usage will be made, the amount of the re-use fee can be specified. Or the re-use fee can be expressed as a percentage of the original fee. Or the original fee can be increased and the grant of rights expanded. If the client will want to make a re-use of a unique image on T-shirts, it would be wise to obtain novelty rights in the initial contract. Another approach would be to seek all rights, but illustrators or photographers object to selling rights which may not be used and for which nothing is presumably being paid. In any case, the fact that usage fees must be paid (and permission obtained) for uses beyond the grant of rights should be kept in mind.

❑ Specify the fee. This would also cover any possible variations in the fee, such as a greater fee for the use of more images or for a greater media exposure than originally planned. (Paragraph 4)

❑ Determine whether sales tax must be paid. Many states provide that the sale of a copyright licence does not transfer tangible property and is not taxable (assuming the physical illustrations or photographs are returned to the creator). However, the sales tax laws vary from state to state and must be checked for the particular state involved.

❑ Any expenses which the designer will reimburse to the illustrator or photographer should be specified to avoid misunderstandings. Some illustrators include expenses in their fee (especially if the expenses are minimal), and the designer can certainly ask that this be done, but many illustrators and virtually all photographers bill separately for expenses. (Paragraph 5)

❑ If expenses are to be reimbursed, consider putting a maximum amount on how much will be reimbursed. Any expenses beyond this amount would have to be absorbed by the illustrator or photographer. This makes sense if the cap is based on an estimate provided by the illustrator or photographer. Or, after receiving an itemized estimate of expenses from the illustrator or photographer, the designer may wish to attach this to the contract and state that expenses shall not exceed those estimates by more than 10 percent without the consent of the designer. (Paragraph 5)

❑ Determine whether the illustrator or photographer marks up expenses, such as billing 15 to 20 percent of the expenses as an additional charge. If expenses are going to be marked up, this should be stated. (Paragraph 5)

❑ If expenses will be significant, consider whether an advance against expenses is justified. If an advance against expenses is given, it should certainly have to be repaid if the expenses are never incurred.

❑ State that payment shall be made within a certain number of days after delivery of the finished art, usually within thirty days after such delivery. Obviously this should be after the date when payment will be received from the client, unless the designer is willing to bear the negative cash flow. (Paragraph 6)

❑ Deal with the issue of payment for work-in-progress that is postponed but not cancelled. A pro rata billing might be appropriate to handle this. (Paragraph 6)

❑ The fee for cancellation of the assignment should be specified. The designer should have the right to stop work on the project without being liable for more than the work done to date by the illustrator or photographer, unless special circumstances have caused the illustrator or photographer to have other losses. Such losses might, for example, be caused by cancellation on such short notice that a photographer is unable to schedule other work. (Paragraph 6)

❑ Specify any advances to be paid against the fee. A schedule of payments might be necessary for an extensive job, in which case the designer might also want advances from the client.

❑ Revisions or reshoots can be a problem. The illustrator or photographer should be given the first opportunity to make revisions or reshoots, after which the designer should be able to change to another illustrator or photographer. (Paragraph 7)

❏ If revisions or reshoots are the fault of the illustrator or photographer, no additional fee should be charged. However, if the designer changes the nature of the assignment, additional fees will be payable. Again, if the designer is making changes because of changes by the client, the designer's contract with the client will have to provide for additional payments. (Paragraph 7)

❏ If the illustrator or photographer is to receive authorship credit, the designer may allow the illustrator or photographer to remove his or her name if changes are done by someone else. (Paragraph 7)

❏ With respect to revisions or the assignment itself, the designer should seek to avoid forcing the illustrator or photographer to rush or work unusual hours since the fees for work under such stress may be higher.

❏ Document any changes in the assignment in writing, since there may later be a question as to whether the changes were executed accurately and whether they came within the initial description of the project. Paragraph 18 requires that all modifications to the agreement be written. Form 9, the Work Change Order Form, can be used as necessary to document changes.

❏ State whether the illustrator or photographer will receive name credit with the image. (Paragraph 8)

❏ State if copyright notice for the photographs or illustrations will appear in the name of the photographer or illustrator when the design is published. (Paragraph 9)

❏ Specify who owns the physical art or transparencies. (Paragraph 10)

❏ Unless there is a special reason to obtain ownership of preliminary materials used to create the design, the ownership of these materials would be retained by the illustrator or photographer. This would include the photographer's outtakes. (Paragraph 10)

❏ The illustrator or photographer must obtain releases with respect both to using copyrighted work or, in some cases, using the images of people. Such releases should protect both the designer and the designer's client. (Paragraph 11)

❏ The designer may want a warranty and indemnity provision, in which the illustrator or photographer states the work is not a copyright infringement and not libelous and agrees to pay for the designer's damages and attorney's fees if this is not true. Such a warranty should not extend to materials provided by the designer for insertion in the book. (Paragraph 12)

❏ Include a provision for arbitration, except as to amounts which can be sued for in small claims court. (Paragraph 13)

❏ Allow the illustrator or photographer the right to assign money payable under the contract, unless there is a particular reason not to do so. (Paragraph 14)

❏ Give the designer the right to assign the contract or rights under the contract. The designer will want to assign rights to the client. (Paragraph 14)

❏ Specify a short term for the agreement. (Paragraph 15)

❏ Allow the designer to terminate if the illustrator or photographer does not meet the project's specifications, falls behind schedule, or becomes insolvent. (Paragraph 15)

❏ Compare the standard provisions in the introductory pages with Paragraph 16.

Other provisions that can be added to Form 23

❏ Noncompetition. If the client is concerned about competitors obtaining a similar look, one solution for the designer is to insist on an all rights contract. The illustrator or photographer would have no right to re-use the work at all. A less extreme solution is to have a noncompetition provision, although even this can be objectionable since the illustrator or photographer cannot risk his or her livelihood by agreeing not to work in a particular style. In any case, a noncompetition provision might read as follows:

Noncompetition. The Supplier agrees not to make or permit any use of the Image or similar images which would compete with or impair the use of the Image by the Designer or its client. The Supplier shall submit any proposed uses of the Images or similar images to the Designer for approval, which approval shall not be unreasonably withheld.

Contract with Illustrator or Photographer

AGREEMENT entered into as of the _____ day of _____, 19 _____, between _____, located at _____ (hereinafter referred to as the "Supplier") and_____, located at _____ (hereinafter referred to as the "Designer") with respect to the creation of certain images (hereinafter referred to as the "Images").

WHEREAS, Supplier is a professional illustrator or photographer of good standing;

WHEREAS, Designer wishes the Supplier to create the Images described more fully herein; and

WHEREAS, Supplier wishes to create such Images pursuant to this Agreement;

NOW, THEREFORE, in consideration of the foregoing premises and the mutual covenants hereinafter set forth and other valuable considerations, the parties hereto agree as follows:

1. **Description.** The Supplier agrees to create the Images in accordance with the following specifications:
   Project title and description of Images _____
   _____
   _____
   Other specifications _____
   _____
   Other services to be rendered by Supplier _____
   _____

2. **Due Date.** The Supplier agrees to deliver the Images within _____ days after the later of the signing of this Agreement or, if the Designer is to provide reference, layouts, or specifications, after the Designer has provided same to the Supplier. If the Designer is to review and approve the work in progress, specify the details here _____

3. **Grant of Rights.** Supplier hereby grants to the Designer the following exclusive rights to use the Images:
   For use as_____
   For the product or publication named_____
   These rights shall be worldwide and for the full life of the copyright and any renewals thereof unless specified to the contrary here_____

4. **Fee.** Designer agrees to pay the following purchase price: $_____ for the usage rights granted. If the fee is variable, it shall be computed as follows_____
   _____

5. **Expenses.** Designer agrees to reimburse the Supplier for expenses incurred in creating the Images, provided that such expenses shall be itemized and supported by invoices, shall not be marked up, and shall not exceed $_____ in total.

6. **Payment.** Designer agrees to pay the Supplier within thirty days of the date of Supplier's billing, which shall be dated as of the date of delivery of the Images. In the event that work is postponed or cancelled at the request of the Designer, the Supplier shall have the right to bill and be paid pro rata for work completed through the date of that request, but the Designer shall have no further liability hereunder.

7. **Revisions or Reshoots.** The Supplier shall be given the first opportunity to make any revisions or reshoots requested by the Designer. If the revisions or reshoots are not due to any fault on the part of the Supplier, an additional fee shall be charged as follows _____.
   If the Supplier objects to any revisions to be made by the Designer, the Supplier shall have the right to have any authorship credit and copyright notice in his or her name removed from the Images.

8. Authorship Credit. Authorship credit in the name of the Supplier ❑ shall ❑ shall not accompany the Images when reproduced.

9. Copyright Notice. Copyright notice in the name of the Supplier ❑ shall ❑ shall not accompany the Images when reproduced.

10. Ownership of Physical Images. The ownership of the physical Images in the form delivered shall be the property of _____. Sketches and any other materials created in the process of making the finished Images shall remain the property of the Supplier, unless indicated to the contrary here _____

11. Releases. The Supplier agrees to obtain releases for any art, photography, or other copyrighted materials to be incorporated by the Supplier into the Images.

12. Warranty and Indemnity. The Supplier warrants and represents that he or she is the sole creator of the Images and owns all rights granted under this Agreement, that the Images are an original creation (except for materials obtained with the written permission of others or materials from the public domain), that the Images do not infringe any other person's copyrights or rights of literary property, nor do they violate the rights of privacy of, or libel, other persons. The Supplier agrees to indemnify and hold harmless the Designer against any claims, judgments, court costs, attorney's fees, and other expenses arising from any alleged or actual breach of this warranty.

13. Arbitration. All disputes arising under this Agreement shall be submitted to binding arbitration before_____ _____ in the following location _____ and settled in accordance with the rules of the American Arbitration Association. Judgment upon the arbitration award may be entered in any court having jurisdiction thereof. Disputes in which the amount at issue is less than $_____ shall not be subject to this arbitration provision.

14. Assignment. The Designer shall have the right to assign any or all of its rights and obligations pursuant to this Agreement. The Supplier shall have the right to assign monies due to him or her under the terms of this Agreement, but shall not make any other assignments hereunder.

15. Term and Termination. This Agreement shall have a term ending _____ months after payment pursuant to Paragraph 6. The Designer may terminate this Agreement at any time prior to the Supplier's commencement of work and may terminate thereafter if the Supplier fails to adhere to the specifications or schedule for the Images. This Agreement shall also terminate in the event of the Supplier's bankruptcy or insolvency. The rights and obligations of the parties pursuant to Paragraphs 3, 8, 9, 10, 11, 12, 13, and 14 shall survive termination of this Agreement.

16. Miscellany. This Agreement constitutes the entire understanding between the parties. Its terms can be modified only by an instrument in writing signed by both parties. A waiver of a breach of any of the provisions of this Agreement shall not be construed as a continuing waiver of other breaches of the same or other provisions hereof. This Agreement shall be binding upon the parties hereto and their respective heirs, successors, assigns, and personal representatives. This Agreement shall be governed by the laws of the State of _____.

IN WITNESS WHEREOF, the parties hereto have signed this Agreement as of the date first set forth above.

Supplier _____   Designer _____
                                                                                          Company Name

By _____
                                                                          Authorized Signatory, Title

Contract with Printer

Clients frequently ask designers not only to design a job, but also to deliver finished printed pieces. Perhaps the job is a simple one, such as a two fold brochure in black and white. Or the job may be complex, involving six-color printing and die-cuts. The basic issues for the designer remain the same: minimizing the risk to the designer's reputation, sanity, and finances while endeavoring to satisfy the client. This section deals with the business and legal ramifications of working with a printer. However, the more the designer learns about the printing process, the greater the likelihood that each job will be a success.

The designer must realistically assess whether he or she is qualified to take the job through the printing process. The production aspects of printing have been dealt with at length in books such as *Pocket Pal* (International Paper Company, P.O.Box 100, Church Street Station, New York, New York 10008-0100) and *Getting It Printed* by Mark Beach, Steve Shepro, and Ken Russon (Coast to Coast Books, distributed by North Light Books). If the designer is not qualified to work with a printer, it might be possible to find an advisor to fill the role of production supervisor. Of course, the printer should be trustworthy enough to ensure proper production techniques and quality, but this is not always the case. Certainly the designer should review samples of the printer's work to see if the quality is satisfactory. However, the designer who is handling the printing is expected by the client to be able to monitor the performance of the printer and make the printer correct the errors that inevitably have to be dealt with in production.

If the designer feels comfortable in agreeing to take the job through the completion of printing, the issue of the scope of the designer's duties must be resolved. Is the designer expected to proof, to be on press, to handle all contacts with the printer, and to make any corrections which are necessary? The scope of duties will be a function of whether the designer or client is most competent in these areas.

If the designer is to handle the printing, a crucial issue is who pays the printer. The designer may want to give a quotation to the client that includes the cost of the printing. This gives the opportunity to make a profit on the printing. In some cases, the profit on the printing can be greater than the design fee.

What happens if, after the job is printed, the client refuses to pay the designer? The designer has a bill from the printer that must be paid. The typical scenario involves a client with (sometimes unreasonably) high standards and a printing job that is "commercially acceptable." This means that the printing is all right, but not of the highest quality. The printer expects the designer to accept the job, yet the designer finds the job is not acceptable to the client. Nor can the designer easily reject the job, since the printer has not made errors that would justify such a rejection.

This nightmare can be avoided in several ways. Some designers simply refuse to handle money in relation to printing. They insist that the client contract directly with the printer, even if the designer is to render services during the printing process. What duties the designer performs are billed to the client on an agreed upon basis, either as a fee, an hourly rate, or a markup. If the designer prefers to pay the printer, the printer must understand and agree to meet a quality standard consistent with the client's expectation (and the designer's agreement with the client).

The first step in dealing with a printer is to request a price quotation. To do this, detailed specifications must be given. It is always wise to seek more than one bid, since prices vary widely. One reason for great price variation is that printers have different equipment. The equipment may make the printer effective for one project but not another, which is reflected in the price. Asking each printer about what they print most efficiently may give helpful insights into selecting the right printer. A helpful guide that lists printers, discusses their merits and demerits, and provides comparison charts, is *Directory of Book, Catalog, and Magazine Printers* by John Kremer (Ad-Lib Publications, P.O. Box 1102, Fairfield, Iowa 52556-1102).

Since the specifications initially given to the printer are always subject to change, estimates often include variable costs for different formats, number of pages, and the size of the print run. Schedule A can be used as a Request for Printing Quotation or, when the job is ready to print, it can be used as Printing Specifications to accompany Form 24. When requesting quotations, always keep the specifications identical for each printer. This may be difficult if, for example, a printer has a special house paper (which is purchased in large quantities to create a cost savings) and bases its bid on such paper. Of course, the designer is free to supply his or her own paper and ink. If this is to be done, it should be indicated in the quotation request. Also, find out how long a quotation will hold before the printer will insist on rebidding the job (and may increase the price).

Once a printer has given an acceptable printing quotation, the designer wants to know that the job will be of appropriate quality and delivered on time. It is important to check the printer's camera work before allowing the job to be printed. This is usually done by reviewing blue lines, color keys, chromalins, or similar proofs. After approval, the printer is free to print in conformity with the approved proofs. Some clients will want the designer or a production specialist on press to watch and approve the print run, especially for color printing.

The printing industry has developed what it calls "trade customs," which are a set of rules intended to govern the relationship of printer to client. Notwithstanding these self-serving rules,

the designer can certainly create his or her own contractual arrangement by having the printer sign a contract with explicit terms such as those contained in Form 24.

The price will usually be expressed as a certain amount for a certain quantity (such as $7,500 for 7,500 brochures). Trade custom allows for the printer to deliver 10 percent more or less than the agreed upon quantity. These "overs" or "unders" are paid for at the marginal unit cost (which might be $.50 apiece, even if the average unit cost is $1, since the initial cost of the film work and setting up the press are not part of the marginal unit cost). If the designer will not accept either overs or unders, this should be stated in the specifications. In such a case the printer will probably adjust its price upward.

The designer will certainly keep ownership over whatever materials he or she gives to the printer, such as mechanicals or art. If these materials are valuable, they should be insured and returned as soon as possible after printing. A more sensitive issue is ownership of the materials created by the printer in the course of the project. If, for whatever reason, the designer wishes to have a future printing done by a different printer, the designer must have the right to receive any film and separations back from the printer. The best way to accomplish this is to own the film, require the printer to store it without charge, and pay only for delivery charges if the designer decides to move the film to another printer. Printers should agree to this, since the film will never have to be moved if they satisfy the designer. At the same time, the designer should also be aware that the client may expect to own what both the designer and the printer create, so this must be resolved in a way consistent with the understanding between designer and printer.

Printers will seek to limit their liability to the amount paid for the printing job. But what if a job costs $10,000 to print, yet the designer loses a $30,000 fee because the printer never delivers or delivers too late? The printer will also prefer to deliver "F.O.B. printing plant," which means that the printer will load the job at the printing plant without charge but has no responsibility after that. The designer will either arrange to pay shipping and insurance costs to the final destination or ask the printer to ship "C.I.F. Bridgeport, Connecticut," if that is the destination. C.I.F. means that a price quotation covers the cost of the merchandise as well as insurance and freight charges to the destination which are paid by the shipping party (in this case, the printer). If the printer does arrange this, it will no doubt want to bill an extra charge. In any case, the designer must be assured that if the job is lost or damaged in shipment, the insurance funds are available to cover the loss and, if feasible, reprint.

If the designer is not handling the job for the client, the client may still be very appreciative if the designer alerts the client to risks in the printing process. Although Form 24 is set up for the designer to contract with and pay the printer, it could as easily be used between the client and the printer.

Filling in the Form

In the Preamble fill in the date and the names and addresses of the parties. In Paragraph 1 check the appropriate box and either fill in the specifications in Paragraph 1 or in Schedule A. For a job with several components to print, more than one copy of Schedule A might be used. In Paragraph 2 specify the delivery date, the place of delivery, and the terms (probably F.O.B. or C.I.F.). In Paragraph 3 restate the number of copies, give the price, indicate the amount of overs and unders which are acceptable, and specify the price per unit for the overs and unders. In Paragraph 4 specify when payment must be made after delivery (usually thirty days for United States printers, although sixty days is sometimes agreed to). In both Paragraph 5 and Paragraph 6 indicate whether the printer must insure the materials and, if so, for how much. In Paragraph 6 also indicate which party will pay the expense of

returning the materials. In Paragraph 8 specify the arbitrator, the place of arbitration, and the amount beneath which claims can be brought in small claims court. In Paragraph 9 specify a term for the contract. In Paragraph 10 indicate which state's laws shall govern the contract. Have both parties sign and append Schedule A, if necessary. Detailed instructions on filling out Schedule A are not included here, because the designer should either be expert enough to fill out that schedule or should use the assistance of a skilled production manager.

Negotiation Checklist

❏ Fill out the specifications to attain the printed piece that the designer wants, including quantity, stock, trim size, number of pages, binding (if any), whether proofs (such as blue lines or color keys) will be provided, packing, and any other specifications. (Paragraph 1 or Schedule A)

❏ Specify a delivery date. (Paragraph 2)

❏ Specify a delivery location. (Paragraph 2)

❏ Indicate the terms of delivery, such as F.O.B. or C.I.F., and be certain the job is sufficiently insured. (Paragraph 2)

❏ State that the risk of loss is borne by the printer until the job is delivered according to the terms of the contract. (Paragraph 2)

❏ State that time is of the essence. The printer will resist this, since late delivery will be an actionable breach of contract. (Paragraph 2)

❏ Do not allow the printer to limit damages for nondelivery or late delivery to the purchase price of the job.

❏ State the price for the quantity ordered. (Paragraph 3)

❏ Specify whether 10 percent overs or unders is acceptable. (Paragraph 3)

❏ Determine whether any sales or other tax must be paid on the printing, and ascertain whether this tax has been included in the price or will be an additional charge. This can be extremely complex, since out of state sales and sales for resale may not require the payment of tax. If there is any doubt, it should be resolved by checking with the sales tax authorities in the printer's, designer's, and client's states.

❏ State when payment will be made after delivery, which is usually within thirty or sixty days. (Paragraph 4)

❏ Do not give the printer a security interest in the job, which the printer might want until full payment has been made. Such a security interest, when perfected by filing with the appropriate government agencies, would give the printer a right to the printed materials or to any sale proceeds from the materials.

❏ State that all materials supplied by the designer remain the property of the designer and must be returned when no longer needed. (Paragraph 5)

❏ Do not give the printer a security interest in materials supplied by the designer.

❏ Indicate that the printer shall pay the expense of returning the materials supplied by the designer. (Paragraph 5)

❏ State whether materials supplied by the designer shall be insured by the printer and, if so, for how much. (Paragraph 5)

❏ State that all materials created by the printer shall be the property of the designer, must be stored without charge, and must be returned when no longer needed. (Paragraph 5)

❏ Indicate who will pay for the return to the designer of materials created by the printer. (Paragraph 5)

❏ State whether materials created by the printer and owned by the designer will be insured by the printer and, if they are to be insured, for how much. (Paragraph 5)

❏ Decide whether the printer may use other companies to do part of the production process. Printers may have color inserts, binding, shrink-wrapping, or other production done by other companies. If the designer's trust is with a particular printer, this practice may be ill-advised. In any case, the designer should be familiar with the true capabilities of the printer. Jobbing work out may cause production delays. Also, a printer's bid which seems too high may be the result of the printer marking up work to be done by others, instead of doing that work itself.

❏ If the printer requests a provision to extend the delivery date in the event of war, strikes, or similar situations beyond its control, the designer should specify that after some period of time the contract will terminate. This period of time might be relatively brief if the job has not yet been printed.

❏ Require proofs for all parts of the job, and hold the printer responsible for matching these proofs. (Paragraph 7)

❏ Require that the printer meet a quality standard reflected in samples shown by the printer.

❏ Do not allow the printer to make a blanket disclaimer of warranties, since these warranties are to protect the buyer. A warranty is a fact the buyer can rely upon, such as the printer's statement that a certain kind of paper will be used or simply the fact that the printer has title to what is printed and can sell it.

❏ The designer should ascertain any extra expenses, such as charges for traps, screens, reverses, knockouts, or other special work; charges for changes in the specifications after an order has been placed; charges to use paper and ink provided by the designer; charges for delays caused by the designer's tardiness in reviewing pre-press proofs; charges for press proofing (that is, having someone review sheets and make adjustments while the press is running); charges for samples to be air freighted or for extra covers; charges for storage of unbound sheets or bound books; charges for shipping; and any other charges.

❏ State that disputes shall be arbitrated, but do not allow the printer either to have the arbitration at its sole option or to specify the location as its place of business. (Paragraph 8)

❏ Specify a short contractual term, such as a period of months. (Paragraph 9)

❏ Allow the designer to terminate without charge prior to the printer's commencement of work or if the printer fails to meet the production specifications or the production schedule. (Paragraph 9)

❏ State that the contract will terminate in the event that the printer becomes bankrupt or insolvent. (Paragraph 9)

❏ Specify that the designer's right to materials it supplied or materials the printer created will survive termination of the contract, as will the right to arbitration. (Paragraph 9)

❏ If there is to be any charge for cancellation of an order, make certain such a charge bears a reasonable relationship to expenses actually incurred by the printer for that order.

❏ If work beyond the original specifications is needed, define a method or standard that the printer will use to bill such extra work.

❏ Do not allow the printer to limit the time to inspect the printed materials and complain about defects, since the designer should certainly have a reasonable amount of time to do this. What is reasonable will depend on the use to which the client will put the materials. Of course, defects should be looked for and documented in writing as soon as discovered.

❏ If at all possible, refuse any provision stating that the designer or client warrants the printed materials are not a copyright infringement, libelous, obscene, or otherwise unlawful, and indemnifies the printer if this is not true. Another variation to be avoided would allow the printer to refuse to complete or deliver the job in the event of a breach of such a warranty.

❏ Review the standard provisions in the introductory pages and compare them with Paragraphs 8 and 10.

Contract with Printer

AGREEMENT entered into as of the _____ day of _____ 19____, between _____ (hereinafter referred to as the "Designer"), located at _____, and _____ (hereinafter referred to as the "Printer"), located at _____ , with respect to the printing of certain materials (hereinafter referred to as the "Work").

WHEREAS, the Designer has prepared the Work for publication and wishes to have the Work printed in accordance with the terms of this Agreement; and

WHEREAS, the Printer is in the business of printing and is prepared to meet the specifications and other terms of this Agreement with respect to printing the Work;

NOW, THEREFORE, in consideration of the foregoing premises and the mutual covenants hereinafter set forth and other valuable consideration, the parties hereto agree as follows:

1. **Specifications.** The Printer agrees to print the Work in accordance with ❑ Schedule A or ❑ the following specifications:

    Title_____

    Description_____

    _____

    _____

    Quantity_____

    Repro Materials_____

    _____

    _____

    Stock_____

    PrePress_____

    Proofs_____

    Binding_____

    Packing_____

    Other specifications_____

    _____

2. **Delivery and Risk of Loss.** Printer agrees to deliver the order on or before _____, 19____ to the following location _____ and pursuant to the following terms _____. The Printer shall be strictly liable for loss, damage, or theft of the order until delivery has been made as provided in this paragraph. Time is of the essence with respect to the delivery date.

3. **Price.** The price for the quantity specified in Paragraph 1 shall be $_____. Overs and unders shall not be acceptable unless specified to the contrary here _____, in which case the price shall be adjusted at the rate of $_____ per thousand.

4. **Payment.** The price shall be payable within _____ days of delivery.

5. **Ownership and Return of Supplied Materials.** All camera-ready copy, artwork, film, separations, and any other materials supplied by the Designer to the Printer shall remain the exclusive property of the Designer and be returned by the Printer at its expense as soon as possible upon the earlier of either the printing of the Work or the Designer's request. The Printer shall be liable for any loss or damage to such materials from the time of receipt

until the time of return receipt by the Designer. The Printer ❏ shall ❏ shall not insure such materials for the benefit of the Designer in the amount of $_____.

6. **Ownership and Return of Commissioned Materials.** All materials created by the Printer for the Designer, including but not limited to sketches, copy, dummies, working mechanical art, type, negatives, positives, flats, plates, or belts, shall become the exclusive property of the Designer and shall be stored without expense by the Printer and be returned at the Designer's request. The expense of such return of materials shall be paid by the ❏ Printer ❏ Designer. The Printer shall be liable for any loss or damage to such materials from the time of creation until the time of return receipt by the Designer. The Printer ❏ shall ❏ shall not insure such materials for the benefit of the Designer in the amount of $_____.

7. **Proofs.** If proofs are requested in the specifications, the Work shall not be printed until such proofs have been approved in writing by the Designer. The finished copies of the Work shall match the quality of the proofs.

8. **Arbitration.** All disputes arising under this Agreement shall be submitted to binding arbitration before _____ _____ at the following location _____ and the arbitration award may be entered for judgment in any court having jurisdiction thereof. Notwithstanding the foregoing, either party may refuse to arbitrate when the dispute is for less than $_____.

9. **Term and Termination.** This Agreement shall have a term ending _____ months after payment pursuant to Paragraph 4. The Designer may terminate this Agreement at any time prior to the Printer's commencement of work and may terminate thereafter if the Printer fails to adhere to the specifications or production schedule for the Work. This Agreement shall also terminate in the event of the Printer's bankruptcy or insolvency. The rights and obligations of the parties pursuant to Paragraphs 5, 6, and 8 shall survive termination of the Agreement.

10. **Miscellany.** This Agreement contains the entire understanding between the parties and may not be modified, amended, or changed except by an instrument in writing signed by both parties. A waiver of any breach of any of the provisions of this Agreement shall not be construed as a continuing waiver of other breaches of the same or other provisions hereof. This Agreement shall be binding upon the parties hereto and their respective heirs, successors, assigns, and personal representatives. This Agreement shall be interpreted under the laws of the State of _____.

IN WITNESS WHEREOF, the parties have signed this Agreement as of the date first set forth above.

Printer_____   Designer_____
              Company Name   Company Name

By_____   By_____
      Authorized Signatory, Title   Authorized Signatory, Title

Schedule A　　　❑ **Request for Printing Quotation**　　　❑ **Printing Specifications**

Printer _____　　Designer _____

Address _____　　Address _____

_____　　_____

Contact Person _____　　Contact Person _____

Phone _____　　Phone _____

Job Name _____　　Job Number _____

Description _____　　Date for Quotation _____

_____　　Date Job to Printer _____

_____　　Date Job Needed _____

Quantity:　1) _____ 2) _____ 3) _____ ❑ Additional _____

Size:　Flat Trim _____ x _____　Folded/ Bound to _____ x _____

　　Number of Pages _____　❑ Self Cover　　❑ Plus Cover　　❑ Cover Bleed

Design includes:　❑ Page Bleeds # _____　　❑ Screen Tints # _____　　❑ Reverses # _____

　Halftones Print:　　❑ Halftone (black) # _____　　❑ Duotone (black plus PMS _____) # _____

　　　　　　　　　Size of Halftones _____

Color Requirements:

　Cover:　　❑ 4 Color Process　❑ Spot Colors PMS #s _____ plus Black

　Inside:　　❑ Full Color　　❑ Spot Color PMS #s _____　❑ Color Signatures only # _____

　Color Separations:　❑ transparencies # _____　❑ reflective art # _____　❑ provided by client

　Original art will be supplied in a:　　❑ scanable form　　❑ rigid form

　Sizes of finished separations _____

　Coatings:　Overall Varnish / Spot Varnish　│　Gloss Varnish / Dull Varnish / Liquid Lamination / UV Coating

	Overall Varnish	Spot Varnish	Gloss Varnish	Dull Varnish	Liquid Lamination	UV Coating
Cover	❑	❑	❑	❑	❑	❑
Inside	❑	❑	❑	❑	❑	❑

　Special instructions _____

_____

_____

Mechanicals:

Color breaks shown: ❏ on acetate overlays   ❏ on tissues   ❏ # of pieces of separate line art _____

Paper Stock: Name   Weight   Grade   Finish   Color

Cover_____   _____   _____   _____   _____

Inside_____   _____   _____   _____   _____

Insert / Other_____   _____   _____   _____   _____

❏ Send samples of paper   ❏ Make book dummy

Other Printing Specifications:

❏ Special Inks _____

❏ Die Cutting   ❏ Embossing   ❏ Engraving   ❏ Foil Stamping   ❏ Thermography   ❏ Serial Numbering

❏ Other _____

_____

Proofs: ❏ Blues   ❏ Color Keys   ❏ Chromalins   ❏ Progressives   ❏ Press Proofs

Details _____

Bindery: ❏ Hard Bound   ❏ Perfect Bound   ❏ Spiral Bound   ❏ Ring Binder   ❏ Saddle Stitch

❏ Score   ❏ Perforate   ❏ Fold   ❏ Drill   ❏ Punch   ❏ Round Corners   ❏ Tip In

Details _____

Packing: ❏ Rubber/String/Paper Band in #_____   ❏ Shrink Wrap in #_____   ❏ Bulk in Cartons

❏ Maximum weight per carton _____lbs   ❏ Skids   ❏ Pallets   ❏ Other _____

Shipping:

Deliver To _____

_____

_____

❏ Truck   ❏ Rail   ❏ Sea   ❏ Air   ❏ Drop Ship   ❏ UPS/Other _____

❏ Customer pick up   ❏ Separate shipping costs   ❏ Send cheapest way   ❏ Other _____

Shipment terms _____   ❏ Insure for _____ percent of printing cost

Miscellaneous instructions: _____

_____

_____

_____

_____

_____

_____

Designer—Sales Agent Contract

FORM
25

Many designers are also illustrators. Form 25 is a contract for use with an agent when the designer is acting as an illustrator. However, designers may legitimately wonder why the practice of having a sales agent does not play a greater role in the field of design. Most designers, when questioned, will say that they obtain work by word of mouth. They do not advertise in promotional books, do direct mail, or make cold calls to potential clients. Few of the promotional books are designed to target the corporate clients likely to be sought by designers. However, designers also feel that appearing to seek work is undignified. Whether such an attitude can survive the 1990s, especially for new designers seeking to establish their businesses, is an issue that each designer will have to face.

Larger design firms may use an employee to develop business through a combination of overtures to potential clients, promotional pieces, sophisticated use of press releases and other types of publicity (such as articles written by or about principals of the firm), and participation in organizations where a designer might meet either clients or peers. Many owners of firms feel that they must be solely responsible for generating business. If an unusual situation were to arise in which an agent were used for the sale of design, Form 25 would provide a framework to create a contract. Of course, each provision would have to be carefully examined. For example, the designer is used to doing billing and servicing accounts. So there would be little reason to give the agent any commission on accounts not obtained directly by the agent. The mix of fees, expenses, and overhead costs would have to be carefully analysed, but it is unlikely that the designer would pay as high a rate of commission to an agent as an illustrator pays. Whether such arrangements will come into existence depends in part on the willingness of clients to deal with someone other than the designer.

In any case, an agent who sells illustration can be of great value to a designer. Instead of seeking illustration assignments, the designer can de-

vote more time to his or her creativity and to seeking design work. The cost to the designer is the agent's commission, which is usually 25 percent, but the hope is that the agent will enable the designer to earn more. The agent may have better contacts and be able to secure a better quality of client and more remunerative assignments.

The agent should not be given markets in which the agent cannot effectively sell. For example, an agent in New York may not be able to sell in Los Angeles or London. Nor should the agent be given exclusivity in markets in which the designer may want to sell or want to have other agents sell. The most important exclusion here is that the agent should not have any rights to commissions with respect to design work. If the agent, by chance, obtains a design assignment, a different fee structure should be used to compensate the agent.

The length of the contract should not be overly long, or should be subject to a right of termination on notice, because if the agent fails to sell the designer must take over sales or find another agent. The agent's promise to use best efforts is almost impossible to enforce.

Promotion is an important aspect of the agent's work for the designer. The designer will have to provide sufficient samples for the agent to work effectively. Beyond this, direct mail campaigns and paid advertising in the promotional directories may gain clients. The sharing of such promotional expenses must be agreed to between the designer and agent.

One sticky issue can be house accounts, which are clients of the designer not obtained by the agent. Both the definition of house accounts and the commission paid to the agent on such accounts must be negotiated. Clearly the designer must not allow design clients to be mixed with illustration clients in dealing with house accounts.

Termination raises another difficult issue, since the agent may feel that commissions should continue to be paid for assignments obtained by the designer after termination from clients originally contacted by the agent. There are several approaches to resolve this. The agent may be given a continuing right to commissions for a limited time depending on how long the representation lasted. Or the designer may make a payout to the agent, either in a lump sum or in installments over several years. If the relationship was brief and unsuccessful, of course, the agent should have no rights at termination except to collect commissions for assignments obtained prior to termination.

The agent would usually handle billings and provide accountings, although the designer may wish to take care of this if staffing permits. The designer would want to be able to review the books and records of the agent. Since both the designer and agent provide personal services, the contract should not be assignable.

A distinction has to be made between an agent obtaining assignments and obtaining a book contract. The agent for an author receives a commission of 10-15 percent, compared to the 25 percent charged by the agent for an illustrator. If an agent arranges an assignment for a book jacket or a limited number of illustrations in a book, the 25 percent commission is reasonable. But if the designer is to be the author or co-author of a book, it might be fairer to reduce the commission to the 10-15 percent range. One consideration might be whether the designer receives a flat fee or a royalty, since a royalty makes the designer more like an author.

A good source to locate agents is the membership list for the Society of Photographer and Artist Representatives (SPAR), P.O. Box 845, FDR Station, New York, New York, 10017.

Filling in the Form

In the Preamble fill in the date and the names and addresses of the designer and agent. In Paragraph 1 indicate the geographical area and markets in which the agent will represent the designer, the types of work covered, and whether the representation will be exclusive or nonexclusive. Be very specific when indicating the type of art or design covered by the contract, since design (and perhaps certain types of illustration) will nor-

mally be excluded from the coverage of the contract and this may require some precision of definition. In Paragraph 4 fill in the length of the term. In Paragraph 5 fill in the commission rates. In Paragraph 6 check the party responsible for billings. In Paragraph 7 indicate the time for payment after receipt of fees and the interest rate for late payments. In Paragraph 8 indicate how promotional expenses will be shared. In Paragraph 11 state when and for how long the agent shall have a right to commissions after termination. In Paragraph 13 give the names of arbitrators and the place for arbitration, as well as filling in the maximum amount which can be sued for in small claims court. In Paragraph 17 fill in which state's laws will govern the contract. Both parties should sign the contract and, if necessary, fill in the Schedule of House Accounts by listing the names and addresses of clients.

Negotiation Checklist

❑ Limit the scope of the agent's representation by geography and types of markets. (Paragraph 1)

❑ Limit the scope of the agent's representation with respect to the nature of the work, including the exclusion of design from the scope of the representation except in unusual cases. (Paragraph 1)

❑ State whether the representation is exclusive or nonexclusive. (Paragraph 1) If the representation is exclusive, the agent will have a right to commissions on assignments obtained by other agents. Assignments obtained by the designer would fall under the House Account provision in Paragraph 5.

❑ If the agent uses other agents for certain markets (for example, for foreign sales or film sales), review the impact of this on the amount of commissions.

❑ State that sales through galleries or sales of original art in general are not within the scope of the agency agreement.

❏ Any rights not granted to the agent should be reserved to the designer. (Paragraph 1)

❏ Require that the agent use best efforts to sell the work of the designer. (Paragraph 2)

❏ Require that the agent shall keep the designer promptly and regularly informed with respect to negotiations and other matters, and shall submit all offers to the designer.

❏ State that any contract negotiated by the agent is not binding unless signed by the designer.

❏ If the designer is willing to give the agent a power of attorney so the agent can sign on behalf of the designer, the power of attorney should be very specific as to what rights the agent can exercise.

❏ Require that the agent keep confidential all matters handled for the designer.

❏ Give the designer the right to accept or reject any assignment which is obtained by the agent. (Paragraph 2)

❏ Specify the amount of samples to be supplied to the agent by the designer. (Paragraph 3)

❏ If the samples are valuable, agree as to their value.

❏ Require the agent to insure the samples at the value agreed to.

❏ Raise the agent's responsibility for the samples to strict liability for any loss or damage.

❏ Provide for a short term, such as one year. (Paragraph 4) This interplays with the termination provision. Since termination is permitted on thirty days notice in Paragraph 11, the length of the term is of less importance in this contract.

❏ If the contract has a relatively long term and cannot be terminated on notice at any time, allow termination if the agent fails to generate a certain level of sales on a quarterly, semiannual, or annual basis.

❏ If the contract has a relatively long term and cannot be terminated on notice at any time, allow for termination if a certain agent dies or leaves the agency.

❏ Specify the commission percentage for assignments obtained by the agent during the term of the contract. This is usually 25 percent of the fee, and may be 2 1/2 to 5 percent higher for out-of-town assignments. (Paragraph 5)

❏ Define house accounts, probably as accounts obtained by other agents prior to the contract or obtained by the designer at any time, and specify the commission to be paid on such accounts. A reasonable commission might be 10 percent, especially if the agent does the billing. The designer may not want to pay any commission on these accounts, while the agent may want the full commission. (Paragraph 5)

❏ List house accounts by name on the Schedule of House Accounts. This can be supplemented if house accounts are developed after the contract is signed. (Paragraph 5)

❏ State that the commission shall be computed on the billing less any expenses incurred by the designer, especially if expenses are substantial and are not reimbursed by the client. (Paragraph 5)

❏ State that commissions are not payable on billings which have not been collected. (Paragraph 5)

❏ Confirm that the agent will not collect a commission for the designer's speaking fees, grants, or prizes.

❏ Distinguish between an assignment to contribute to a book and being the author or coauthor of a book. Agents representing authors charge 10-15 percent of proceeds from the book as the commission. While the dividing line may be a fine one, designers likely to make substantial contributions to a book should consider whether treatment as an author may be appropriate in terms of the agent's commission rate. (Paragraph 5)

❏ In the case of an agent for a book, consider letting the agency do only that particular title or project.

❏ Determine who will bill and collect from the client. This would usually be a service provided by the agent, but a design firm is likely to be more capable of handling this than an individual illustrator. (Paragraph 6)

❏ If the agent is collecting billings, give the designer the right to collect his or her share directly from clients. This might provide some protection against the agent's insolvency or holding of money in the event of a dispute.

❏ Require payments to be made quickly after billings are collected. (Paragraph 7)

❏ Charge interest on late payments, but avoid a usurious interest rate. (Paragraph 7)

❏ Require the agent to treat money due the designer as trust funds and hold it in an account separate from accounts for the funds of the agency. (Paragraph 7)

❏ Share promotional expenses, such as direct mail campaigns or paid page advertising in directories. The agent may contribute 25 percent or more to these expenses. (Paragraph 8)

❏ State that both parties must agree before promotional expenses may be incurred by the agent. (Paragraph 8)

❏ Require the agent to pay for a specified minimum amount of promotional expenses, perhaps without any sharing on the part of the designer.

❏ If expenses incurred by the agent benefit several designers (or illustrators), be certain there is a fair allocation of expenses to each designer.

❏ Require the agent to bear miscellaneous marketing expenses, such as messengers, shipping, and the like. (Paragraph 8)

❏ If the agent insists that the designer bear certain expenses, require the designer's approval for expenses in excess of a minimum amount.

❏ If the agent is billing, state that the designer shall receive a copy of the invoice given to the client. (Paragraph 9)

❏ Provide for full accountings on a regular basis, such as every six months, if requested. (Paragraph 9)

❏ Give a right to inspect books and records on reasonable notice. (Paragraph 10)

❏ Allow for termination on thirty days notice to the other party. (Paragraph 11)

❏ State that the agreement will terminate in the event of the agent's bankruptcy or insolvency. (Paragraph 11)

❏ Specify for how long, if at all, the agent will receive commissions from assignments obtained by the designer from clients developed by the agent during the time the contract was in effect. (Paragraph 11) For example, if the agency contract lasted for less than a year, the agent might have such a right for 3 months after termination. If the agency contract lasted more than a year but less than two years, the right might continue for 6 months after termination. If the agent has a right to commissions after termination for too long a period, the designer may find it difficult to find another agent.

❏ Do not give the agent any rights to commissions from house accounts after termination.

❑ For book contracts, it is customary for the agent to continue to collect royalties and deduct the agent's commission even after termination of the agency contract. However, it would be better for the designer to have the right to direct payment of his or her share after such termination.

❑ Instead of allowing the agent to collect commissions for some period of time after termination, a fixed amount might be stated in the original contract. For example, 20 percent of the average annual billings for the prior three years might be payable in 3 installments over a year. The percentages and payment schedule are negotiable, but the designer must avoid any agreement which would make it difficult either to earn a living or find another agent. The percentage to be paid might increase if the agent has represented the designer for a longer period (or decrease for a shorter period), but should be subject to a cap or maximum amount.

❑ Do not allow assignment of the contract, since both the agent and the designer are rendering personal services. (Paragraph 12)

❑ Allow the designer to assign payments due to him or her under the contract. (Paragraph 12)

❑ If the agent represents creators who are competitive with one another, decide what precautions might be taken against favoritism. Whether it is advantageous or disadvantageous to have an agent represent competing talent will depend on the unique circumstances of each case.

❑ If the agent requires a warranty and indemnity clause under which the designer states that he or she owns the work and has the right to sell it, limit the liability of the designer to actual breaches resulting in a judgment and try to place a maximum amount on the potential liability.

❑ Provide for arbitration of disputes in excess of the amount which can be sued for in small claims court. (Paragraph 13)

❑ If there is an arbitration provision, consider specifying the Joint Ethics Committee in New York City or a similar group near the designer's location to act as arbitrator.

❑ Compare the standard provisions in the introductory pages with Paragraphs 14-17.

Designer—Sales Agent Contract

AGREEMENT, entered into as of this _____ day of _____, 19_____, between _____ (hereinafter referred to as the "Designer"), located at _____, and _____ (hereinafter referred to as the "Agent"), located at _____;

WHEREAS, the Designer is an established designer of proven talents; and

WHEREAS, the Designer wishes to have an agent represent him or her in marketing certain rights enumerated herein; and

WHEREAS, the Agent is capable of marketing the work produced by the Designer; and

WHEREAS, the Agent wishes to represent the Designer;

NOW, THEREFORE, in consideration of the foregoing premises and the mutual covenants hereinafter set forth and other valuable consideration, the parties hereto agree as follows:

1. **Agency**. The Designer appoints the Agent to act as his or her representative:

    (A) in the following geographical area _____

    (B) for the following markets:

    ❏ Advertising   ❏ Corporate   ❏ Book Publishing   ❏ Magazines

    ❏ Other, specified as _____

    (C) for the following types of art or design_____

    (D) to be the Designer's ❏ exclusive ❏ nonexclusive agent for the area, markets, and types of work indicated.

    Any rights not granted to the Agent are reserved to the Designer.

2. **Best Efforts.** The Agent agrees to use his or her best efforts in submitting the Designer's work for the purpose of securing assignments for the Designer. The Agent shall negotiate the terms of any assignment that is offered, but the Designer may reject any assignment if he or she finds the terms thereof unacceptable.

3. **Samples.** The Designer shall provide the Agent with such samples of work as are from time to time necessary for the purpose of securing assignments. These samples shall remain the property of the Designer and be returned on termination of this Agreement. The Agent shall take reasonable efforts to protect the work from loss or damage, but shall be liable for such loss or damage only if caused by the Agent's negligence.

4. **Term.** This Agreement shall take effect as of the date first set forth above, and remain in full force and effect for a term of _____, unless terminated as provided in Paragraph 11.

5. **Commissions.** The Agent shall be entitled to the following commissions: **(A)** On assignments obtained by the Agent during the term of this Agreement, _____ percent of the billing. **(B)** On house accounts, _____ percent of the billing. For purposes of this Agreement, house accounts are defined as accounts obtained by the Designer at any time or obtained by another agent representing the Designer prior to the commencement of this Agreement and are listed in the Schedule of House Accounts attached to this Agreement. **(C)** For books which the Designer authors or coauthors, _____ percent of the royalties or licensing proceeds paid to the Designer by the publisher or its licensees.

    It is understood by both parties that no commissions shall be paid on assignments rejected by the Designer or for which the Designer fails to receive payment, regardless of the reason payment is not made. Further, no commissions shall be payable in either **(A)** or **(B)** above for any part of the billing that is due to expenses incurred by the Designer in performing the assignment, whether or not such expenses are reimbursed by the client. In the event that a flat fee is paid by the client, it shall be reduced by the amount of expenses incurred by the Designer in performing the assignment, and the Agent's commission shall be payable only on the fee as reduced for expenses.

6. **Billing.** The ❏ Designer ❏ Agent shall be responsible for all billings.

7. **Payments.** The party responsible for billing shall make all payments due within _____ days of receipt of any fees covered by this Agreement. Such payments due shall be be deemed trust funds and shall not be inter-mingled with funds belonging to the party responsible for billing and payment. Late payments shall be accom-panied by interest calculated at the rate of _____ percent per month thereafter.

8. **Promotional Expenses.** Promotional expenses, including but not limited to promotional mailings and paid advertising, shall be mutually agreed to by the parties and paid _____ percent by the Agent and _____ per-cent by the Designer. The Agent shall bear the expenses of shipping, insurance, and similar marketing expenses.

9. **Accountings.** The party responsible for billing shall send copies of invoices to the other party when rendered. If requested, that party shall also provide the other party with semiannual accountings showing all assignments for the period, the clients' names and addresses, the fees paid, expenses incurred by the Designer, the dates of payment, the amounts on which the Agent's commissions are to be calculated, and the sums due less those amounts already paid.

10. **Inspection of the Books and Records.** The party responsible for the billing shall keep the books and records with respect to payments due each party at his or her place of business and permit the other party to inspect these books and records during normal business hours on the giving of reasonable notice.

11. **Termination.** This Agreement may be terminated by either party by giving thirty (30) days written notice to the other party. If the Designer receives assignments after the termination date from clients originally obtained by the Agent during the term of this Agreement, the commission specified in Paragraph 5(A) shall be payable to the Agent under the following circumstances. If the Agent has represented the Designer for _____ months or less, the Agent shall receive a commission on such assignments received by the Designer within _____ days of the date of termination. This period shall increase by thirty (30) days for each additional _____ months that the Agent has represented the Designer, but in no event shall such period exceed _____ days. In the event of the bankruptcy or insolvency of the Agent, this Agreement shall also terminate. The rights and obligations under Paragraphs 3, 6, 7, 8, 9, and 10 shall survive termination.

12. **Assignment.** This Agreement shall not be assigned by either of the parties hereto, except that the Designer shall have the right to assign any monies due the Designer under this Agreement.

13. **Arbitration.** Any disputes arising under this Agreement shall be settled by arbitration before _____ under the rules of the American Arbitration Association in the City of _____, except that the par-ties shall have the right to go to court for claims of $_____ or less. Any award rendered by the arbitrator may be entered in any court having jurisdiction thereof.

14. **Notices.** All notices shall be given to the parties at their respective addresses set forth above.

15. **Independent Contractor Status.** Both parties agree that the Agent is acting as an independent contractor. This Agreement is not an employment agreement, nor does it constitute a joint venture or partnership between the Designer and Agent.

16. **Amendments, Mergers, Successors and Assigns.** All amendments to this Agreement must be written. This Agreement incorporates the entire understanding of the parties. It shall be binding on and inure to the benefit of the successors, administrators, executors, or heirs of the Agent and Designer.

17. **Governing Law.** This Agreement shall be governed by the laws of the State of _____.

IN WITNESS WHEREOF, the parties have signed this Agreement as of the date set forth above.

Designer_____   Agent_____
　　　　　　　Company name　　　　　　　　　　　　　　　　　Company name

By_____   By_____
　　　　Authorized Signatory, Title　　　　　　　　　　　　Authorized Signatory, Title

Schedule of House Accounts

Date_____

1._____
(name and address of client)

2._____

3._____

4._____

5._____

6._____

7._____

8._____

9._____

10._____

11._____

12._____

13._____

14._____

15._____

16._____

17._____

18._____

19._____

20._____

Designer's Lecture Contract

Many designers find lecturing to be both a source of income and a rewarding opportunity to express their feelings about their work and being an designer. High schools, colleges, conferences, professional societies, and other institutions often invite designers to lecture. Slides of the designs may be used during these lectures and, in some cases, an exhibition may be mounted during the designer's visit.

A contract ensures that everything goes smoothly. For example, who should pay for slides that the designer has to make for that particular lecture? Who will pay for transportation to and from the lecture? Who will supply materials for a demonstration of technique? Will the designer have to give one lecture in a day or, as the institution might prefer, many more? Will the designer have to review portfolios of students? Resolving these kinds of questions, as well as the amount of and time to pay the fee, will make any lecture a more rewarding experience.

Filling in the Form

In the Preamble give the date and the names and addresses of the parties. In Paragraph 1 give the dates when the designer will lecture, the nature and extent of the services the designer will perform, and the form in which the designer is to bring examples of his or her work. In Paragraph 2 specify the fee to be paid to the designer and when it will be paid during the designer's visit. In Paragraph 3 give the amounts of expenses to be paid (or state that none or all of these expenses are to be paid), specify which expenses other than travel and food and lodging are covered, and show what will be provided by the sponsor (such as food or lodging). In Paragraph 10 indicate which state's law will govern the contract. Then have both parties sign the contract. On the Schedule of Designs, list the works to be brought to the lecture and their insurance value.

Negotiation Checklist

❑ How long will the designer be required to stay at the sponsoring institution in order to perform the required services? (Paragraph 1)

❑ What are the nature and extent of the services the designer will be required to perform? (Paragraph 1)

❑ What slides, original designs, or other materials must the designer bring? (Paragraph 1)

❑ Specify the work facilities which the sponsor will provide the designer. (Paragraph 2)

❑ Specify the fee to be paid to the designer. (Paragraph 2)

❑ Give the time to pay the fee. (Paragraph 2)

❑ Require part of the fee be paid in advance.

❑ Specify the expenses which will be paid by the sponsor, including the time for payment of these expenses. (Paragraph 3)

❑ Indicate what the sponsor may provide in place of paying expenses, such as giving lodging, meals, or a car. (Paragraph 3)

❑ If illness prevents the designer from coming to lecture, state that an effort will be made to find another date. (Paragraph 4)

❑ If the sponsor must cancel for a reason beyond its control, indicate that the expenses incurred by the designer must be paid and there will be an attempt to reschedule. (Paragraph 4)

❑ If the sponsor cancels within 48 hours of the time designer is to arrive, consider requiring the full fee as well as expenses be paid.

❏ Provide for the payment of interest on late payments by the sponsor. (Paragraph 5)

❏ Retain for the designer all rights, including copyrights, in any recordings of any kind which may be made of designer's visit. (Paragraph 6)

❏ If the sponsor wishes to use a recording of the designer's visit, such as a video, require that the sponsor obtain the designer's written permission and that, if appropriate, a fee be negotiated for this use. (Paragraph 6)

❏ Provide that the sponsor is strictly responsible for loss or damage to any designs from the time they leave the designer's studio until they are returned there. (Paragraph 7)

❏ Require the sponsor to insure the designs and specify insurance values. (Paragraph 7)

❏ Consider which risks may be excluded from the insurance coverage.

❏ Consider whether the designer should be the named beneficiary of the insurance coverage for his or her works.

❏ Provide who will pay the cost of packing and shipping the works to and from the sponsor. (Paragraph 8)

❏ Provide who will take the responsibility to pack and ship the works to and from the sponsor.

❏ Compare the standard provisions in the introductory pages with Paragraphs 9-10.

Designer's Lecture Contract

AGREEMENT, dated the _____ day of _____, 19 ____, between_____
(hereinafter referred to as the "Designer"), located at _____and
_____(hereinafter referred to as the "Sponsor"),
located at _____.

WHEREAS, the Sponsor is familiar with and admires the work of the Designer; and

WHEREAS, the Sponsor wishes the Designer to visit the Sponsor to enhance the opportunities for its students to have contact with working professional designer; and

WHEREAS, the Designer wishes to lecture with respect to his or her work and perform such other services as this contract may call for;

NOW, THEREFORE, in consideration of the foregoing premises and the mutual covenants hereinafter set forth and other valuable considerations, the parties hereto agree as follows:

1. Designer to Lecture. The Designer hereby agrees to come to the Sponsor on the following date(s):_____
_____ and perform the following services:
_____.
The Designer shall use best efforts to make his or her services as productive as possible to the Sponsor. The Designer further agrees to bring examples of his or her own work in the form of _____
_____.

2. Payment. The Sponsor agrees to pay as full compensation for the Designer's services rendered under Paragraph 1 the sum of $_____. This sum shall be payable to the Designer on completion of the _____ day of the Designer's residence with the Sponsor.

3. Expenses. In addition to the payments provided under Paragraph 2, the Sponsor agrees to reimburse the Designer for the following expenses:

(A) Travel expenses in the amount of $_____.

(B) Food and lodging expenses in the amount of $_____.

(C) Other expenses listed here:_____in the amount of $_____.

The reimbursement for travel expenses shall be made fourteen (14) days prior to the earliest date specified in Paragraph 1. The reimbursement for food, lodging, and other expenses shall be made at the date of payment specified in Paragraph 2, unless a contrary date is specified here:_____.

In addition, the Sponsor shall provide the Designer with the following:

(A) Tickets for travel, rental car, or other modes of transportation as follows: _____
_____

(B) Food and lodging as follows: _____
_____

(C) Other hospitality as follows: _____
_____

4. Inability to Perform. If the Designer is unable to appear on the dates scheduled in Paragraph 1 due to illness, the Sponsor shall have no obligation to make any payments under Paragraphs 2 and 3, but shall attempt to reschedule the Designer's appearance at a mutually acceptable future date. If the Sponsor is prevented from having the Designer appear by Acts of God, hurricane, flood, governmental order, or other cause beyond its control, the Sponsor shall be responsible only for the payment of such expenses under Paragraph 3 as the Designer shall have actually incurred. The Sponsor agrees in such a case to attempt to reschedule the Designer's appearance at a mutually acceptable future date.

5. Late Payment. The Sponsor agrees that, in the event it is late in making payment of amounts due to the Designer under Paragraphs 2, 3, or 8, it will pay as additional liquidated damages _____ percent in interest on the amounts it is owing to the Designer, said interest to run from the date stipulated for payment in Paragraphs 2, 3, or 8 until such time as payment is made.

6. Copyrights and Recordings. Both parties agree that the Designer shall retain all rights, including copyrights, in relation to recordings of any kind made of the appearance or any works shown in the course thereof. The term "recording" as used herein shall include any recording made by electrical transcription, tape recording, wire recording, film, videotape, or other similar or dissimilar methods of recording, whether now known or hereinafter developed. No use of any such recording shall be made by the Sponsor without the written consent of the Designer and, if stipulated therein, additional compensation for such use.

7. Insurance and Loss or Damage. The Sponsor agrees that it shall provide wall-to-wall insurance for the works listed on the Schedule of Designs for the values specified therein. The Sponsor agrees that it shall be fully responsible and have strict liability for any loss or damage to the designs from the time said designs leaves the Designer's residence or studio until such time as it is returned there.

8. Packing and Shipping. The Sponsor agrees that it shall fully bear any costs of packing and shipping necessary to deliver the works specified in Paragraph 7 to the Sponsor and return them to the Designer's residence or studio.

9. Modification. This contract contains the full understanding between the parties hereto and may only be modified in a written instrument signed by both parties.

10. Governing Law. This contract shall be governed by the laws of the State of _____.

IN WITNESS WHEREOF, the parties hereto have signed this Agreement as of the date first set forth above.

Designer_____   Sponsor_____
                                                                    Company Name

                                               By_____
                                                            Authorized Signatory, Title

Schedule of Designs

	Title	Medium	Size	Value
1.				
2.				
3.				
4.				
5.				
6.				
7.				

Licensing Contract to Merchandise Designs

Licensing is the granting of rights to use designs created by the designer on posters, calendars, greeting cards and stationery, apparel, wall paper, mugs and other household items, or any of innumerable other applications. Needless to say, this can be very lucrative for the designer. So many of the products used in everyday life depend on visual qualities to make them attractive to purchasers. These qualities may reside in the design of the product itself or in the use of designs on the product. For the designer to enter the world of manufactured, mass-produced goods offers the opportunity for new audiences and new modes of production and distribution. The best guide for designers on the subject of licensing is *Licensing Art & Design* by Caryn Leland (Allworth Press, distributed by North Light Books). The potentially large sums of money involved, as well as the possible complexity of licensing agreements, make *Licensing Art & Design* a valuable resource for designers who either are licensing designs or would like to enter the field of licensing.

Form 27, the Licensing Contract to Merchandise Designs, is adapted from a short-form licensing agreement which appears in *Licensing Art & Design.*

Filling in the Form

In the Preamble fill in the date and the names and addresses of the parties. In Paragraph 1 indicate whether the rights are exclusive or nonexclusive, give the name and description of the image, state what types of merchandise the image can be used for, specify the geographical area for distribution, and limit the term of the distribution. In Paragraph 3 specify the advance, if any, and the royalty percentage. State the date on which payments and statements of account are to begin in Paragraph 4. Indicate the number of samples to be given to the designer in Paragraph 6. In Para-

graph 13 specify which state's laws will govern the contract. Give addresses for correspondence relating to the contract in Paragraph 14. Have both parties sign the contract.

Negotiation Checklist

❑ Carefully describe the image to be licensed. (Paragraph 1)

❑ State whether the rights given to the licensee are exclusive or nonexclusive. (Paragraph 1)

❑ Indicate which kinds of merchandise the image is being licensed for. (Paragraph 1)

❑ State the area in which the licensee may sell the licensed products. (Paragraph 1)

❑ Give a term for the licensing contract. (Paragraph 1)

❑ Reserve all copyrights in the image to the designer. (Paragraph 2)

❑ Require that credit and copyright notice in the designer's name appear on all licensed products. (Paragraph 2)

❑ Require that credit and copyright notice in the designer's name appear on packaging, advertising, displays, and all publicity.

❑ Have the right to approve packaging, advertising, displays, and publicity.

❑ Give the licensee the right to use the designer's name and, in an appropriate case, picture, provided that any use must be to promote the product using the image and must be in dignified taste.

❏ Determine whether the royalty should be based on retail price or, as is more commonly the case, on net price which is what the manufacturer actually receives. (Paragraph 3)

❏ If any expenses are to reduce the amount on which royalties are calculated, these expenses must be specified.

❏ Specify the royalty percentage. (Paragraph 3)

❏ Require the licensee to pay an advance against royalties to be earned. (Paragraph 3)

❏ Indicate that any advance is nonrefundable. (Paragraph 3)

❏ Require minimum royalty payments for the term of the contract, regardless of sales.

❏ Require monthly or quarterly statements of account accompanied by any payments which are due. (Paragraph 4)

❏ Specify the information to be contained in the statement of account, such as units sold, total revenues received, special discounts, and the like. (Pragraph 4)

❏ Give the designer a right to inspect the books and records of the licensee. (Paragraph 5)

❏ Provide that if an inspection of the books and records uncovers an error to the disadvantage of the designer and that error is more than 5 percent of the amount owed designer, then the licensee shall pay for the cost of the inspection and any related costs.

❏ Provide for a certain number of samples to be given to the designer by the manufacturer. (Paragraph 6)

❏ Give the designer a right to purchase additional samples at manufacturing cost or, at least, at no more than the price paid by wholesalers. (Paragraph 6)

❏ Consider whether the designer will want the right to sell the products at retail price, rather than being restricted to using the samples and other units purchased for personal use.

❏ Give the designer a right of approval over the quality of the reproductions to protect the designer's reputation. (Paragraph 7)

❏ Require the licensee give best efforts to promoting the licensed products. (Paragraph 8)

❏ Specify and amount of money that the licensee must spend on promotion.

❏ Specify the type of promotion that the licensee will provide.

❏ Reserve all rights to the designer which are not expressly transferred. (Paragraph 9)

❏ If the licensee's usage may create trademarks or other rights in the product, it is important that these rights be owned by the designer after termination of the license.

❏ Require the licensee to indemnify the designer for any costs arising out of the use of the image on the licensed products. (Paragraph 10)

❏ Have the licensee provide liability insurance with the designer as a named beneficiary to protect against defects in the products.

❏ Forbid assignment by the licensee, but let the designer assign royalties. (Paragraph 11)

❏ Specify the grounds for terminating the contract, such as the bankruptcy or insolvency of the licensee, failure of the licensee to obey the terms of the contract, cessation of manufacture of the product, or insufficent sales of the licensed products. (This partially covered in Paragraph 4.)

❏ Compare the standard provisions in the introductory pages with Paragraphs 10-15.

Licensing Contract to Merchandise Designs

AGREEMENT made this _____ day of _____, 19_____, between _____ (hereinafter referred to as the "Designer"), located at _____ and _____ (hereinafter referred to as the "Licensee"), located at _____ with respect to the use of a certain design created by the Designer (hereinafter referred to as the "Design") for manufactured products (hereinafter referred to as the "Licensed Products").

WHEREAS, the Designer is a professional designer of good standing; and

WHEREAS, the Designer has created the Design which the Designer wishes to license for purposes of manufacture and sale; and

WHEREAS, the Licensee wishes to use the Design to create a certain product or products for manufacture and sale; and

WHEREAS, both parties want to achieve the best possible quality to generate maximum sales;

NOW, THEREFORE, in consideration of the foregoing premises and the mutual covenants hereinafter set forth and other valuable consideration, the parties hereto agree as follows:

1. **Grant of Merchandising Rights.** The Designer grants to the Licensee the ❏ exclusive ❏ nonexclusive right to use the Design, titled _____ and described as _____, which was created and is owned by the Designer, as or as part of the following type(s) of merchandise:_____ _____ for manufacture, distribution, and sale by the Licensee in the following geographical area:_____ _____ and for the following period of time: _____.

2. **Ownership of Copyright.** The Designer shall retain all copyrights in and to the Design. The Licensee shall identify the Designer as the creator of the Design on the Licensed Products and shall reproduce thereon a copyright notice for the Designer which shall include the word "Copyright" or the symbol for copyright, the Designer's name, and the year date of first publication.

3. **Advance and Royalties.** Licensee agrees to pay Designer a nonrefundable advance in the amount of $_____ upon signing this Agreement, which advance shall be recouped from first royalties due hereunder. Licensee further agrees to pay Illustrator a royalty of _____ (_____ %) percent of the net sales of the Licensed Products. "Net Sales" as used herein shall mean sales to customers less prepaid freight and credits for lawful and customary volume rebates, actual returns, and allowances. Royalties shall be deemed to accrue when the Licensed Products are sold, shipped, or invoiced, whichever first occurs.

4. **Payments and Statements of Account.** Royalty payments shall be paid monthly on the first day of each month commencing _____, 19 _____, and Licensee shall with each payment furnish Designer with a monthly statement of account showing the kinds and quantities of all Licensed Products sold, the prices received therefor, and all deductions for freight, volume rebates, returns, and allowances. The Illustrator shall have the right to terminate this Agreement upon thirty (30) days notice if Licensee fails to make any payment required of it and does not cure this default within said thirty (30) days, whereupon all rights granted herein shall revert immediately to the Illustrator.

5. **Inspection of Books and Records.** Designer shall have the right to inspect Licensee's books and records concerning sales of the Licensed Products upon prior written notice.

6. Samples. Licensee shall give the Designer _____ samples of the Licensed Products for the Designer's personal use. The Designer shall have the right to purchase additional samples of the Licensed Products at the Licensee's manufacturing cost.

7. Quality of Reproductions. The Designer shall have the right to approve the quality of the reproduction of the Design on the Licensed Products, and the Designer agrees not to withhold approval unreasonably.

8. Promotion. Licensee shall use its best efforts to promote, distribute, and sell the Licensed Products.

9. Reservation of Rights. All rights not specifically transferred by this Agreement are reserved to the Designer.

10. Indemnification. The Licensee shall hold the Designer harmless from and against any loss, expense, or damage occasioned by any claim, demand, suit, or recovery against the Designer arising out of the use of the Image for the Licensed Products.

11. Assignment. Neither party shall assign rights or obligations under this Agreement, except that the Designer may assign the right to receive money due hereunder.

12. Nature of Contract. Nothing herein shall be construed to constitute the parties hereto joint venturers, nor shall any similar relationship be deemed to exist between them.

13. Governing Law. This Agreement shall be construed in accordance with the laws of _____; Licensee consents to the jurisdiction of the courts of _____.

14. Addresses. All notices, demands, payments, royalty payments, and statements shall be sent to the Designer at the following address _____ and to the Licensee at _____.

15. Modifications in Writing. This Agreement constitutes the entire agreement between the parties hereto and shall not be modified, amended, or changed in any way except by a written agreement signed by both parties hereto.

IN WITNESS WHEREOF, the parties have signed this Agreement as of the date first set forth above.

Designer_____   Licensee_____
     Company Name   Company Name

By_____   By_____
     Authorized Signatory, Title   Authorized Signatory, Title

Release Form for Models

Designs often portray people. Whether these images are created by the designer or by photographers or illustrators, the designer must be aware of individual's rights to privacy and publicity. While the intricacies of these laws can be reviewed in *Legal Guide for the Visual Artist*, this summary will help alert the designer to potential dangers.

The right to privacy can take a number of forms. For example, it is forbidden by state laws and court decisions to use a person's name, portrait, or picture for purposes of advertising or trade. This raises the question of the definitions for advertising and trade. It would also violate the right of privacy to bring before the public an image which showed or implied something embarrassing and untrue about someone. And physically intruding into private spaces such as a home, perhaps to take a photograph for use as a reference, can be an invasion of privacy.

The right of publicity is the right which a celebrity creates in his or her name, image, and voice. To use the celebrity's image for commercial gain violates this right of publicity. And, while the right of privacy generally protects only living people, a number of states have enacted laws to protect the publicity rights of celebrities even after death. These state laws supplement court decisions which held that celebrities who exploited the commercial value of their names and images while alive had publicity rights after death.

On the other hand, use of people's images for newsworthy and editorial purposes is protected by the First Amendment. No releases need be obtained for such uses which serve the public interest.

What should the designer do about all this? The wisest course is to obtain a model release from anyone who will be recognizable in a design, including people who can be recognized from parts of their body other than the face. Even if the initial use of the design is editorial and does not create a privacy issue, there is always the possibility that an image will be reproduced in other ways such as for posters, postcards, and T-shirts, all of which are clearly trade uses, or for advertising. Only by having a model release can the designer guarantee the right to exploit the commercial value of the image in the future (subject, of course, to the agreement with the photographer or illustrator who may have created the image).

If the designer is creating the image, Form 28 allows the designer (and others who obtain the designer's permission, such as clients) to use the model's image for advertising and trade. The designer should insist that a form like Form 28 also be used by photographers or illustrators working for the designer (and extend the coverage of the release to the designer and his or her clients). While some states may not require written releases or the payment of money for a release, it is always wise to use a written release and make at least a small payment as consideration. By the way, Form 28 is intended for use with friends and acquaintances who pose as well as with professional models.

If the release is drafted to cover one use, but the image is then used in a distorted and embarrassing way for a different purpose, the release may not protect the designer regardless of what it says. For example, a model signed a model release for a bookstore's advertisement in which she was to appear in bed reading a book. This advertisement was later changed and used by a bedsheet manufacturer known for its salacious advertisements. The title on the book became pornographic and a leering old man was placed next to the bed looking at the model. This invaded the model's privacy despite her having signed a release.

In general, a minor must have a parent or guardian give consent. While the designer should check the law in his or her state, the age of majority in most states is eighteen.

The designer should be certain to obtain the release when the image is received (or created), since it is easy to forget if left for later. Also, releases should kept systematically so that they can be related to the design in which the person appears who gave the release. A simple numbering system can be used to connect the releases to the designs. While a witness isn't a necessity, having one can help if a question is later raised about the validity of the release.

If the designer is given a release form to use by a client, the designer must make certain that the form protects the designer. The Negotiation Checklist will be helpful in reviewing any form provided to the designer and suggesting changes to strengthen the form.

Filling in the Form

Fill in the dollar amount being paid as consideration for the release. Then fill in the name of the model and the name of the designer. Have the model and a witness sign the form. Obtain the addresses for both the model and the witness and date the form. If the model is a minor, have the parent or guardian sign. Have the witness sign and give the addresses of the witness and the parent or guardian as well as the date.

Negotiation Checklist

❑ Be certain that some amount of money, even a token amount, is actually paid as consideration for the release.

❑ Have the release be given not only to the designer, but also to the designer's estate and anyone else the designer might want to assign rights to such as a client or a manufacturer of posters or T-shirts.

❑ If the release is obtained by a photographer or illustrator, be certain that the release extends to the designer and his or her clients.

❑ Likewise, it the release form is provided by a client, be certain its coverage offers protection for the designer.

❑ Recite that the grant is irrevocable.

❑ Cover use of the name as well as the image of the person.

❑ Include the right to use the image in all forms, media, and manners of use.

❑ Include the right to make distorted or changed versions of the image as well as composite images.

❑ Allow advertising and trade uses.

❑ Allow any other lawful use.

❑ Have the model waive any right to review the finished artwork, including written copy to accompany the artwork.

❑ Have the model recite that he or she is of full age.

❑ If the model is a minor, have a parent or guardian sign the release.

Release Form for Models

In consideration of _____ Dollars ($_____), receipt of which is acknowledged, I, _____, do hereby give _____, his or her assigns, licensees, and legal representatives the irrevocable right to use my name (or any fictional name), picture, portrait, or photograph in all forms and media and in all manners, including composite or distorted representations, for advertising, trade, or any other lawful purposes, and I waive any right to inspect or approve the finished version(s), including written copy that may be created in connection therewith. I am of full age.* I have read this release and am fully familiar with its contents.

Witness_____   Model_____

Address_____   Address_____

Date _____, 19 ___

——————————————————— Consent (if applicable) ———————————————————

I am the parent or guardian of the minor named above and have the legal authority to execute the above release. I approve the foregoing and waive any rights in the premises.

Witness_____   Parent or Guardian_____

Address_____   Address_____

Date _____, 19 ___

* Delete this sentence if the subject is a minor. The parent or guardian must then sign the consent.

Property Release

Property does not have rights of privacy or publicity. A public building, a horse running in a field, or a bowl of fruit are all freely available to be portrayed in a design.

Nonetheless, there may be times when the designer will want to obtain a release for the use of property belonging to others (or have a photographer or illustrator obtain such a release, in the case of work done on assignment). This might include personal property, such as jewelry or clothing, or the interiors of private buildings, especially if admission is charged. The most important reason for the release is to have a contract which details the terms of use of the property.

If the designer is lent property to use in a work, it is important to obtain a release if the designer has any intention of using that artwork in some way other than the commission. For example, if an designer were hired to create a Christmas card with the image of the client's favorite dog on the front of the card, it would be a breach of an implied provision of the contract for the designer to then sell that image to a manufacturer of dog food for use as product packaging. Such a use would require the owner's permission, which could be obtained by using Form 29.

As with releases for models, property releases should be obtained at the time the property is used and payment, even if only a token payment, should be made to the owner of the property. If a form is supplied by either the client or a photographer or illustrator, be certain its coverage protects the designer.

Filling in the Form

Fill in the amount being paid for use of the property, as well as the name and address of the owner and the name of the designer. Then specify the property which will be used. Finally have both parties sign the release, obtain a witness to each signature (if possible), and give the date.

Negotiation Checklist

❑ Make some payment, however small, as consideration for the release.

❑ Be certain the release runs in favor of the designer's assigns (such as clients) and estate as well as the designer.

❑ If the release is provided by the client, be certain it protects the designer.

❑ If the release is obtained by a photographer or illustrator, be certain its coverage extends to the designer and the designer's clients.

❑ State that the release is irrevocable.

❑ Include the right to copyright and publish the image made from the property.

❑ Include the right to use the image in all forms, media, and manners of use.

❑ Permit advertising and trade uses as well as any other lawful use.

❑ State that the owner has full and sole authority to give the release.

❑ Obtain the right to make distorted versions of the image as well as composite images.

❑ Allow use of the owner's name or a fictional name with the image of the property.

❑ Permit color or black and white images, as well as any type of derivative work.

❑ Have the owner waive any right to review the finished artwork, including written copy to accompany the artwork.

❑ Make certain the owner is of full age and has the capacity to give the release.

Property Release

In consideration of the sum of _____Dollars ($_____),

receipt of which is hereby acknowledged, I, _____,

located at _____, do irrevocably authorize

_____, his or her assigns, licensees, heirs, and legal representatives, to copyright, publish, and use in all forms and media and in all manners for advertising, trade, or any other lawful purpose, images of the following property which I own and have full and sole authority to license for such uses: _____

_____,

regardless of whether said use is composite or distorted in character or form, whether said use is made in conjunction with my own name or with a fictitious name, or whether said use is made in color or otherwise or other derivative works are made through any medium.

I waive any right that I may have to inspect or approve the finished version(s), including written copy that may be used in connection therewith.

I am of full age and have every right to contract in my own name with respect to the foregoing matters. I have read the above authorization and release prior to its execution and I am fully cognizant of its contents.

Witness_____   Owner_____

Address_____   Date_____,19_____

Permission Form

Many projects require obtaining permission from the owners of copyrighted materials such as graphics, photographs, paintings, articles, or excerpts from books. The designer ignores obtaining such permissions at great peril. Not only is it unethical to use someone else's work without permission, it can also lead to liability for copyright infringement.

Of course, some copyrighted works have entered the public domain, which means that they can be freely copied by anyone. For works published by United States authors on or before December 31, 1977, the maximum term of copyright protection was 75 years. If such a work is more than 75 years old, it should be in the public domain in the United States (but may have a different term of protection in other countries). Works published before December 31, 1977 also had an initial term of 28 years and then a renewal term. If the copyright was not renewed, the work would also have gone into the public domain. The Copyright Office can review its records to determine whether a copyright was renewed.

For works published on or after January 1, 1978, the term of protection is usually the life of the author plus 50 years, so these works would only be in the public domain if copyright notice had been omitted or improper. This complicated topic is discussed fully in *Legal Guide for the Visual Artist*. The absence of a copyright notice on works published between January 1, 1978 and February 28, 1989 (when the United States joined the Berne Copyright Union) does not necessarily mean the work is in the public domain. On or after March 1, 1989, copyright notice is no longer required to preserve copyright protection, although such notice does confer some benefits under the copyright law. A basic rule is to obtain permission for using any work, unless the designer is certain the work is in the public domain or determines that the planned use would be a fair use.

Fair use offers another way in which the designer may avoid having to obtain a permission, even though the work is protected by a valid copyright. The copyright law states that copying "for purposes such as criticism, comment, news reporting, teaching (including multiple copies for classroom use), scholarship, or research, is not an infringement of copyright." To evaluate whether a use is a fair use depends on four factors set forth in the law: "(1) the purpose and character of the use, including whether such use is of a commercial nature or is for nonprofit educational purposes; (2) the nature of the copyrighted work; (3) the amount and substantiality of the portion used...and (4) the effect of the use upon the potential market for or value of the copyrighted work." These guidelines have to be applied on a case-by-case basis. If there is any doubt, it is best to seek permission to use the work.

One obstacle to obtaining permissions is locating the person who owns the rights. A good starting point, of course, is to contact the publisher of the material, since the publisher may have the right to grant permissions. If the creator's address is available, the creator can be contacted directly. In some cases, permissions may have to be obtained from more than one party. Creator's societies and agents may be helpful in tracking down the owners of rights.

For an hourly fee, the Copyright Office will search its records to aid in establishing the copyright status of a work. Copyright Office Circular R22, "How to Investigate the Copyright Status of a Work," explains more fully what the Copyright Office can and cannot do. Circulars and forms can be ordered from the Copyright Office by calling (202) 707-9100.

Permissions can be time-consuming to obtain, so starting early in a project is wise. A log should be kept of each request for a permission. In the log, each request is given a number. The log describes the material to be used, lists the name and address of the owner of the rights, shows when the request was made and when any reply was received, indicates if a fee must be paid, and includes any special conditions required by the owner.

Fees may very well have to be paid for certain permissions. If the client is to pay these fees, the designer should certainly specify this in the contract with the client. If the client (such as a publisher) has an agreement making the designer liable if lawsuits arise over permissions which should have been obtained by the designer, the designer should resist such a provision or at least limit the amount of liability. For example, the designer might limit his or her liability to the amount of the design fee paid (but this will not stop the designer being named as a defendant by the owner of the work which was infringed). In any case, the designer should keep in mind that permission fees are negotiable and vary widely in amount. For a project that will require many permissions, advance research as to the amount of the fees is a necessity.

Filling in the Form

The form should be accompanied by a cover letter requesting that two copies of the form be signed and one copy returned. The name and address of the designer, the type of use, and the name of the designer's client, should be filled in. Then the nature of the material should be specified, such as text, photograph, illustration, poem, and so on. The source should be described along with an exact description of the material. If available, fill in the date of publication, the publisher, and the author. Any copyright notice or credit line to accompany the material should be shown. State after Other Provisions any special limitations on the rights granted and also indicate the amount of any fee to be paid. If all the rights are not controlled by the person giving the permission, then that person will have to indicate who else to contact. If more than one person must approve the permission, make certain there are enough signature lines. If the rights are owned by a corporation, add the company name and the title of the authorized signatory. A stamped, self-addressed envelope and a photocopy of the material to be used might make a speedy response more likely.

Negotiation Checklist

❑ State that the permission extends not only to the designer, but also to the designer's successors and assigns. Certainly the permission must extend to the designer's client.

❑ Describe the material to be used carefully, including a photocopy if that would be helpful.

❑ Obtain the right to use the material in future editions, derivations, or revisions of the book or other product, as well as in the present version.

❑ State that nonexclusive world rights in all languages are being granted.

❑ In an unusual situation, seek exclusivity for certain uses of the material. This form does not seek exclusivity.

❑ Negotiate a fee, if requested. Whether a fee is appropriate, and its amount, will depend on whether the project is likely to earn a substantial return.

❑ If a fee is paid, add a provision requiring the party giving the permission to warrant that the material does not violate any copyright or other rights and to indemnify the designer against any losses caused if the warranty is incorrect.

❑ Keep a log on all correspondence relating to permission forms and be certain one copy of each signed permission has been returned for the designer's files.

Permission Form

The Undersigned hereby grant(s) permission to _____ (hereinafter

referred to as the "Designer"), located at _____ , and

to the Designer's successors and assigns, to use the material specified in this Permission Form for the following

book or other product _____

for use by the following publisher or client _____ .

This permission is for the following material:

Nature of material _____

Source _____

Exact description of material, including page numbers_____

If published, date of publication _____

Publisher _____

Author(s) _____

This material may be used for the book or product named above and in any future revisions, derivations, or editions thereof, including nonexclusive world rights in all languages.

It is understood that the grant of this permission shall in no way restrict republication of the material by the Undersigned or others authorized by the Undersigned.

If specified here, the material shall be accompanied on publication by a copyright notice as follows_____

_____

and a credit line as follows _____ .

Other provisions, if any: _____

If specified here, the requested rights are not controlled in their entirety by the Undersigned and the following owners must be contacted: _____

_____

One copy of this Permission Form shall be returned to the Designer and one copy shall be retained by the Undersigned.

_____   _____
Authorized Signatory   Date

_____   _____
Authorized Signatory   Date

Nondisclosure Agreement for Submitting Ideas

What can be more frustrating than having a great idea and not being able to share it with anyone? Especially if the idea has commercial value, sharing it is often the first step on the way to realizing the remunerative potential of the concept. The designer wants to show the idea to a client, publisher, manufacturer, or producer. But how can the idea be protected?

Ideas are not protected by copyright, because copyright only protects the expression of an idea. The idea to create a design which includes an image of the White House is not copyrightable, while the design itself certainly is protected by copyright. The idea to have a television series in which each program would have a designer teach at a well-known landmark in his or her locale is not copyrightable, but each program would be protected by copyright. Of course, copyright is not the only form of legal protection. An idea might be patentable or lead to the creation of a trademark, but these are less likely cases and certainly require expert legal assistance. How does a designer disclose an idea for an image, a format, a product, or other creations without risking that the other party will simply steal the idea?

This can be done by the creation of an express contract, an implied contract (revealed by the course of dealing between the parties), or a fiduciary relationship (in which one party owes a duty of trust to the other party). Form 31, the Nondisclosure Agreement, creates an express contract between the party disclosing the idea and the party receiving it. Form 31 is adapted from a letter agreement in *Licensing Art & Design* by Caryn Leland (Allworth Press, distributed by North Light Books).

What should be done if a company refuses to sign a nondisclosure agreement or, even worse, has its own agreement for the designer to sign? Such an agreement might say that the company will not be liable for using a similar idea and will probably place a maximum value on the idea (such as a few hundred dollars). At this point, the designer has to evaluate the risk. Does the company have a good reputation or is it notorious for appropriating ideas? Are there other companies willing to sign a nondisclosure agreement that could be approached with the idea? If not, taking the risk may make more sense than never exploiting the idea at all. A number of steps, set out in the negotiation checklist, should then be taken to try and gain some protection. The designer will have to make these evaluations on a case-by-case basis.

Filling in the Form

In the Preamble fill in the date and the names and addresses of the parties. In Paragraph 1 describe the information to be disclosed without giving away what it is. Have both parties sign the agreement.

Negotiation Checklist

❏ Disclose what the information concerns without giving away what is new or innovative. For example, "an idea for a new format for a series to teach design" might interest a producer but would not give away the idea of using different designers teaching at landmarks in different locales. (Paragraph 1)

❏ State that the recipient is reviewing the information to decide whether to embark on commercial exploitation. (Paragraph 2)

❏ Require the recipient to agree not to use or transfer the information. (Paragraph 3)

❏ State that the recipient receives no rights in the information. (Paragraph 3)

❏ Require the recipient to keep the information confidential. (Paragraph 4)

❏ State that the recipient acknowledges that disclosure of the information would cause irreparable harm to the designer. (Paragraph 4)

❏ Require good faith negotiations if the recipient wishes to use the information after disclosure. (Paragraph 5)

❏ Allow no use of the information unless agreement is reached after such negotiations. (Paragraph 5)

If the designer wishes to disclose the information despite the other party's refusal to sign the designer's nondisclosure form, the designer should take a number of steps:

❏ First, before submission, the idea should be sent to a neutral third party (such as a notary public or professional design society) to be held in confidence.

❏ Anything submitted should be marked with copyright and trademark notices, when appropriate. For example, the idea may not be copyrightable, but the written explanation of the idea certainly is. The copyright notice could be for that explanation, but might make the recipient more hesitant to steal the idea.

❏ If an appointment is made, confirm it by letter in advance and sign any log for visitors.

❏ After any meeting, send a letter which covers what happened at the meeting (including any disclosure of confidential information and any assurances that information will be kept confidential) and, if at all possible, have any proposal or followup from the recipient be in writing.

Nondisclosure Agreement for Submitting Ideas

AGREEMENT, entered into as of this _____ day of _____, 19___, between_____ (hereinafter referred to as the "Designer"), located at _____, and _____ (hereinafter referred to as the "Recipient"), located at _____.

WHEREAS, the Designer has developed certain valuable information, concepts, ideas, or designs, which the Designer deems confidential (hereinafter referred to as the "Information"); and

WHEREAS, the Recipient is in the business of using such Information for its projects and wishes to review the Information; and

WHEREAS, the Designer wishes to disclose this Information to the Recipient; and

WHEREAS, the Recipient is willing not to disclose this Information, as provided in this Agreement.

NOW, THEREFORE, in consideration of the foregoing premises and the mutual covenants hereinafter set forth and other valuable considerations, the parties hereto agree as follows:

1. **Disclosure.** Designer shall disclose to the Recipient the Information, which concerns:_____ _____

2. **Purpose.** Recipient agrees that this disclosure is only for the purpose of the Recipient's evaluation to determine its interest in the commercial exploitation of the Information.

3. **Limitation on Use.** Recipient agrees not to manufacture, sell, deal in, or otherwise use or appropriate the disclosed Information in any way whatsoever, including but not limited to adaptation, imitation, redesign, or modification. Nothing contained in this Agreement shall be deemed to give Recipient any rights whatsoever in and to the Information.

4. **Confidentiality.** Recipient understands and agrees that the unauthorized disclosure of the Information by the Recipient to others would irreparably damage the Designer. As consideration and in return for the disclosure of this Information, the Recipient shall keep secret and hold in confidence all such Information and treat the Information as if it were the Recipient's own proprietary property by not disclosing it to any person or entity.

5. **Good Faith Negotiations.** If, on the basis of the evaluation of the Information, Recipient wishes to pursue the exploitation thereof, Recipient agrees to enter into good faith negotiations to arrive at a mutually satisfactory agreement for these purposes. Until and unless such an agreement is entered into, this nondisclosure Agreement shall remain in force.

6. **Miscellany.** This Agreement shall be binding upon and shall inure to the benefit of the parties and their respective legal representatives, successors, and assigns.

IN WITNESS WHEREOF, the parties have signed this Agreement as of the date first set forth above.

Designer_____   Recipient_____
                                                           Company Name

                                                         By_____
                                                           Authorized Signatory, Title

Copyright Transfer Form

The copyright law defines a transfer of copyright as an assignment "of a copyright or of any of the exclusive rights comprised in a copyright, whether or not it is limited in time or place of effect, but not including a nonexclusive license." A transfer is, in some way, exclusive. The person receiving a transfer has a right to do what no one else can do. For example, the transfer might be of the right to make copies of the work in the form of posters for distribution in the United States for a period of one year. While this transfer is far less than all rights in the copyright, it is nonetheless exclusive within its time and place of effect.

Any transfer of an exclusive right must be in the form of a writing signed either by the owner of the rights being conveyed or by the owner's authorized agent. While not necessary to make the assignment valid, notarization of the signature is *prima facie* proof that the assignment was signed by the owner or agent.

Form 32 can be used in a variety of situations. If the designer wanted to receive back rights which the designer had transferred in the past, the designer could take an all rights transfer. If the designer enters into a contract involving the transfer of an exclusive right, the parties may not want to reveal all the financial data and other terms contained in the contract. Form 31 could then be used as a short form to be executed along with the contract for the purpose of recordation in the Copyright Office. The assignment in Form 32 should conform exactly to the assignment in the contract itself.

Recordation of copyright transfers with the Copyright Office can be quite important. Any transfer should be recorded within thirty days if executed in the United States, or within sixty days if executed outside the United States. Otherwise, a later conflicting transfer, if recorded first and taken in good faith without knowledge of the earlier transfer, will prevail over the earlier transfer. Simply put, if the same exclusive rights are sold twice and the first buyer doesn't record the transfer, it is quite possible that the second buyer who does record the transfer will be found to own the rights.

Any document relating to a copyright, whether a transfer of an exclusive right or only a nonexclusive license, can be recorded with the Copyright Office. Such recordation gives constructive notice to the world about the facts in the document recorded. Constructive notice means that a person will be held to have knowledge of the document even if, in fact, he or she did not know about it. Recordation gives constructive notice only if the document (or supporting materials) identifies the work to which it pertains so that the recorded document will be revealed by a reasonable search under the title or registration number of the work and registration has been made for the work.

Another good reason to record exclusive transfers is that a nonexclusive license, whether recorded or not, can have priority over a conflicting exclusive transfer. If the nonexclusive license is written and signed and was taken before the execution of the transfer or taken in good faith before recordation of the transfer and without notice of the transfer, it will prevail over the transfer.

A fee must be paid to record documents. Once paid, the Register of Copyrights will record the document and return a certificate of recordation.

Filling in the Form

Give the name and address of the party giving the assignment (the assignor) and the name and address of the party receiving the assignment. Specify the rights transferred. Describe the work or works by title, registration number, and the nature of the work. Date the transfer and have the assignor sign it. If the assignor is a corporation, use a corporate form for the signature.

Negotiation Checklist

❏ Be certain that consideration (something of value, whether a promise or money) is actually given to the other party.

❏ Have the transfer benefit the successors in interest of the assignee.

❏ If the designer is making the transfer, limit the rights transferred as narrowly as possible.

❏ Describe the works as completely as possible, including title, registration number, and the nature of the work.

❏ Have the assignor or the authorized agent of the assignor sign the assignment.

❏ Notarize the assignment to gain the presumption the signature is valid.

❏ If the assignment is to the designer, such as an assignment back to the designer of rights previously conveyed, an all rights provision can be used. (See other provisions)

Other provisions that can be added to Form 32:

❏ Rights transferred. When indicating the rights transferred, the following provision could be used if the designer is to receive all rights. Obviously, the designer should avoid giving such an assignment of rights to another party.

Rights Transferred. All right, title, and interest, including any statutory copyright together with the right to secure renewals and extensions of such copyright throughout the world, for the full term of said copyright or statutory copyright and any renewal or extension of same that is or may be granted throughout the world.

Copyright Transfer Form

FOR VALUABLE CONSIDERATION, the receipt of which is hereby acknowledged, _____ (hereinafter referred to as the "Assignor"), located at _____, does hereby transfer and assign to _____, located at _____, his or her heirs, executors, administrators, and assigns, the following rights: _____ _____ in the copyrights

in the works described as follows:

Title	Registration Number	Nature of Work
_____	_____	_____
_____	_____	_____
_____	_____	_____
_____	_____	_____
_____	_____	_____

IN WITNESS WHEREOF, the Assignor has executed this instrument on the _____ day of _____, 19____.

Assignor_____

Application for Copyright Registration of Designs

To register an artwork or design, the designer must send a completed Form VA, a nonrefundable filing fee, and a nonreturnable deposit portraying the work to be registered. These three items should be sent together to the Register of Copyrights, Copyright Office, Library of Congress, Washington, D.C. 20559. If the designer is working with a piece that is predominantly textual, Form TX is used for the registration.

The instructions for filling in Form VA are provided by the Copyright Office and are reproduced here with Form VA.

The Copyright Office also makes available a free Copyright Information Kit. This includes copies of Form VA and other Copyright Office circulars and is worth requesting. To expedite receiving forms or circulars, the Forms and Circulars Hotline number can be used: (202) 707-9100. Request the kit for the visual arts.

Because of budget constraints, the Copyright Office will accept reproductions of Form VA such as the tear-out form in this book. If the designer wishes to make copies, however, the copies must be clear, legible, on a good grade of white paper, and printed on a single sheet of paper so that when the sheet is turned over the top of page 2 is directly behind the top of page 1. Also, the Register of Copyrights has requested an increase in the fees paid to the Copyright Office, so the fee structure should be checked from time to time.

It is wise to register any work which the designer feels may be infringed. Registration has a number of values, the most important of which is to establish proof that a particular design was created by the designer as of a certain date. Both published and unpublished designs can be registered. In fact, unpublished designs can be registered in groups for a single application fee.

For published designs, the proper deposit is usually two complete copies of the work. For unpublished designs, one complete copy would be correct. Since the purpose of registering is to protect what the designer has created, it is important that the material deposited fully show what is copyrightable.

Obviously unique artworks or designs cannot be sent along with the application for purposes of identifying themselves, so the Copyright Office accepts other identifying materials. These are usually photographs, photostats, slides, drawings, or other two-dimensional representations of the work. The designer should provide as much identifying material as is necessary to show the copyrightable content of the design, including any copyright notice which has been used. The proper form for copyright notice, by the way, is © or Copyright or Copr., the designer's name, and the year of first publication.

The preferable size for identifying materials (other than transparencies) is 8-by-10 inches, but anything from 3-by-3 inches up to 9-by-12 inches will be acceptable. Also, at least one piece of the identifying material must give an exact measurement of one or more dimensions of the design and give the title on its front, back, or mount.

For a full review of registration and its requirements, the designer can consult Copyright Office Circular 40, *Copyright Registration for Works of the Visual Arts*, and Circular 40a, *Deposit Requirements of Claims to Copyright in Visual Arts Material*.

A copyright registration is effective as of the date that the Copyright Office receives the application, fee, and deposit materials in an acceptable form, regardless of how long it takes to send back the certificate of registration. It may take 120 days before the certificate of registration is sent to the designer. To know whether the Copyright Office received the materials, they can be sent by registered or certified mail with a return receipt requested from the post office.

A designer can request information as to the status of an application. However, a fee will be charged by the Copyright Office if such a status report must be given within twenty days of the submission of the application.

For a more extensive discussion of the legal aspects of copyright, the designer can consult *Legal Guide for the Visual Artist* or *Make It Legal* by Lee Wilson (Allworth Press, distributed by North Light Books).

⊘ Filling Out Application Form VA

Detach and read these instructions before completing this form. Make sure all applicable spaces have been filled in before you return this form.

BASIC INFORMATION

When to Use This Form: Use Form VA for copyright registration of published or unpublished works of the visual arts. This category consists of "pictorial, graphic, or sculptural works," including two-dimensional and three-dimensional works of fine, graphic, and applied art, photographs, prints and art reproductions, maps, globes, charts, technical drawings, diagrams, and models.

What Does Copyright Protect? Copyright in a work of the visual arts protects those pictorial, graphic, or sculptural elements that, either alone or in combination, represent an "original work of authorship." The statute declares: "In no case does copyright protection for an original work of authorship extend to any idea, procedure, process, system, method of operation, concept, principle, or discovery, regardless of the form in which it is described, explained, illustrated, or embodied in such work."

Works of Artistic Craftsmanship and Designs: "Works of artistic craftsmanship" are registrable on Form VA, but the statute makes clear that protection extends to "their form" and not to "their mechanical or utilitarian aspects." The "design of a useful article" is considered copyrightable "only if, and only to the extent that, such design incorporates pictorial, graphic, or sculptural features that can be identified separately from, and are capable of existing independently of, the utilitarian aspects of the article."

Labels and Advertisements: Works prepared for use in connection with the sale or advertisement of goods and services are registrable if they contain "original work of authorship." Use Form VA if the copyrightable material in the work you are registering is mainly pictorial or graphic; use Form TX if it consists mainly of text. **NOTE:** Words and short phrases such as names, titles, and slogans cannot be protected by copyright, and the same is true of standard symbols, emblems, and other commonly used graphic designs that are in the public domain. When used commercially, material of that sort can sometimes be protected under state laws of unfair competition or under the Federal trademark laws. For information about trademark registration, write to the Commissioner of Patents and Trademarks, Washington, D.C. 20231.

Deposit to Accompany Application: An application for copyright registration must be accompanied by a deposit consisting of copies representing the entire work for which registration is to be made.

> **Unpublished Work:** Deposit one complete copy.

> **Published Work:** Deposit two complete copies of the best edition.

> **Work First Published Outside the United States:** Deposit one complete copy of the first foreign edition.

> **Contribution to a Collective Work:** Deposit one complete copy of the best edition of the collective work.

The Copyright Notice: For works first published on or after March 1, 1989, the law provides that a copyright notice on a specified form "may be placed on all publicly distributed copies from which the work can be visually perceived." Use of the copyright notice is the responsibility of the copyright owner and does not require advance permission from the Copyright Office. The required form of the notice for copies generally consists of three elements: (1) the symbol "©", or the word "Copyright," or the abbreviation "Copr."; (2) the year of first publication; and (3) the name of the owner of copyright. For example: "© 1989 Jane Cole." The notice is to be affixed to the copies "in such manner and location as to give reasonable notice of the claim of copyright." Works first published prior to March 1, 1989, **must** carry the notice or risk loss of copyright protection.

For information about notice requirements for works published before March 1, 1989, or other copyright information, write: Information Section, LM-401, Copyright Office, Library of Congress, Washington, D.C. 20559.

PRIVACY ACT ADVISORY STATEMENT Required by the Privacy Act of 1974 (P.L. 93-579)

The authority for requesting this information is title 17, U.S.C., secs. 409 and 410. Furnishing the requested information is voluntary. But if the information is not furnished, it may be necessary to delay or refuse registration and you may not be entitled to certain relief, remedies, and benefits provided in chapters 4 and 5 of title 17, U.S.C.

The principal uses of the requested information are the establishment and maintenance of a public record and the examination of the application for compliance with legal requirements.

Other routine uses include public inspection and copying, preparation of public indexes, preparation of public catalogs of copyright registrations, and preparation of search reports upon request.

NOTE: No other advisory statement will be given in connection with this application. Please keep this statement and refer to it if we communicate with you regarding this application.

LINE-BY-LINE INSTRUCTIONS

1 SPACE 1: Title

Title of This Work: Every work submitted for copyright registration must be given a title to identify that particular work. If the copies of the work bear a title (or an identifying phrase that could serve as a title), transcribe that wording *completely* and *exactly* on the application. Indexing of the registration and future identification of the work will depend on the information you give here.

Previous or Alternative Titles: Complete this space if there are any additional titles for the work under which someone searching for the registration might be likely to look, or under which a document pertaining to the work might be recorded.

Publication as a Contribution: If the work being registered is a contribution to a perodical, serial, or collection, give the title of the contribution in the "Title of This Work"space. Then, in the line headed "Publication as a Contribution," give information about the collective work in which the contribution appeared.

Nature of This Work: Briefly describe the general nature or character of the pictorial, graphic, or sculptural work being registered for copyright. Examples: "Oil Painting"; "Charcoal Drawing"; "Etching"; "Sculpture"; "Map"; "Photograph"; "Scale Model"; "Lithographic Print"; "Jewelry Design"; "Fabric Design."

2 SPACE 2: Author(s)

General Instructions: After reading these instructions, decide who are the "authors" of this work for copyright purposes. Then, unless the work is a "collective work," give the requested information about every "author" who contributed any appreciable amount of copyrightable matter to this version of the work. If you need further space, request additional Continuation Sheets. In the case of a collective work, such as a catalog of paintings or collection of cartoons by various authors, give information about the author of the collective work as a whole.

Name of Author: The fullest form of the author's name should be given. Unless the work was "made for hire," the individual who actually created the work is its "author." In the case of a work made for hire, the statute provides that "the employer or other person for whom the work was prepared is considered the author."

What is a "Work Made for Hire"? A "work made for hire" is defined as: (1) "a work prepared by an employee within the scope of his or her employment"; or (2) "a work specially ordered or commissioned for use as a contribution to a collective work, as a part of a motion picture or other audiovisual work, as a translation, as a supplementary work, as a compilation, as an instructional text, as a test, as answer material for a test, or as an atlas, if the parties expressly agree in a written instrument signed by them that the work shall be considered a work made for hire." If you have checked "Yes" to indicate that the work was "made for hire," you must give the full legal name of the employer (or other person for whom the work was prepared). You may also include the name of the employee along with the name of the employer (for example: "Elster Publishing Co., employer for hire of John Ferguson").

"Anonymous" or "Pseudonymous" Work: An author's contribution to a work is "anonymous" if that author is not identified on the copies or phonorecords of the work. An author's contribution to a work is "pseudonymous" if that author is identified on the copies or phonorecords under a fictitious name. If the work is "anonymous" you may: (1) leave the line blank; or (2) state "anonymous" on the line; or (3) reveal the author's identity. If the work is "pseudonymous" you may: (1) leave the line blank; or (2) give the pseudonym and identify it as such (for example: "Huntley Haverstock, pseudonym"); or (3) reveal the author's name, making clear which is the real name and which is the pseudonym (for example: "Henry Leek, whose pseudonym is Priam Farrel"). However, the citizenship or domicile of the author **must** be given in all cases.

Dates of Birth and Death: If the author is dead, the statute requires that the year of death be included in the application unless the work is anonymous or pseudonymous. The author's birth date is optional, but is useful as a form of identification. Leave this space blank if the author's contribution was a "work made for hire."

Author's Nationality or Domicile: Give the country of which the author is a citizen, or the country in which the author is domiciled. Nationality or domicile **must** be given in all cases.

Nature of Authorship: Give a brief general statement of the nature of this particular author's contribution to the work. Examples: "Painting"; "Photograph"; "Silk Screen Reproduction"; "Co-author of Cartographic Material"; "Technical Drawing"; "Text and Artwork."

3 SPACE 3: Creation and Publication

General Instructions: Do not confuse "creation" with "publication." Every application for copyright registration must state "the year in which creation of the work was completed." Give the date and nation of first publication only if the work has been published.

Creation: Under the statute, a work is "created" when it is fixed in a copy or phonorecord for the first time. Where a work has been prepared over a period of time, the part of the work existing in fixed form on a particular date constitutes the created work on that date. The date you give here should be the year in which the author completed the particular version for which registration is now being sought, even if other versions exist or if further changes or additions are planned.

Publication: The statute defines "publication" as "the distribution of copies or phonorecords of a work to the public by sale or other transfer of ownership, or by rental, lease, or lending"; a work is also "published" if there has been an "offering to distribute copies or phonorecords to a group of persons for purposes of further distribution, public performance, or public display." Give the full date (month, day, year) when, and the country where, publication first occurred. If first publication took place simultaneously in the United States and other countries, it is sufficient to state "U.S.A."

4 SPACE 4: Claimant(s)

Name(s) and Address(es) of Copyright Claimant(s): Give the name(s) and address(es) of the copyright claimant(s) in this work even if the claimant is the same as the author. Copyright in a work belongs initially to the author of the work (including, in the case of a work made for hire, the employer or other person for whom the work was prepared). The copyright claimant is either the author of the work or a person or organization to whom the copyright initially belonging to the author has been transferred.

Transfer: The statute provides that, if the copyright claimant is not the author, the application for registration must contain "a brief statement of how the claimant obtained ownership of the copyright." If any copyright claimant named in space 4 is not an author named in space 2, give a brief, general statement summarizing the means by which that claimant obtained ownership of the copyright. Examples: "By written contract"; "Transfer of all rights by author"; "Assignment"; "By will." Do not attach transfer documents or other attachments or riders.

5 SPACE 5: Previous Registration

General Instructions: The questions in space 5 are intended to find out whether an earlier registration has been made for this work and, if so, whether there is any basis for a new registration. As a rule, only one basic copyright registration can be made for the same version of a particular work.

Same Version: If this version is substantially the same as the work covered by a previous registration, a second registration is not generally possible unless: (1) the work has been registered in unpublished form and a second registration is now being sought to cover this first published edition; or (2) someone other than the author is identified as copyright claimant in the earlier registration, and the author is now seeking registration in his or her own name. If either of these two exceptions apply, check the appropriate box and give the earlier registration number and date. Otherwise, do not submit Form VA; instead, write the Copyright Office for information about supplementary registration or recordation of transfers of copyright ownership.

Changed Version: If the work has been changed, and you are now seeking registration to cover the additions or revisions, check the last box in space 5, give the earlier registration number and date, and complete both parts of space 6 in accordance with the instructions below.

Previous Registration Number and Date: If more than one previous registration has been made for the work, give the number and date of the latest registration.

6 SPACE 6: Derivative Work or Compilation

General Instructions: Complete space 6 if this work is a "changed version," "compilation," or "derivative work," and if it incorporates one or more earlier works that have already been published or registered for copyright, or that have fallen into the public domain. A "compilation" is defined as "a work formed by the collection and assembling of preexisting materials or of data that are selected, coordinated, or arranged in such a way that the resulting work as a whole constitutes an original work of authorship." A "derivative work" is "a work based on one or more preexisting works." Examples of derivative works include reproductions of works of art, sculptures based on drawings, lithographs based on paintings, maps based on previously published sources, or "any other form in which a work may be recast, transformed, or adapted." Derivative works also include works "consisting of editorial revisions, annotations, or other modifications" if these changes, as a whole, represent an original work of authorship.

Preexisting Material (space 6a): Complete this space **and** space 6b for derivative works. In this space identify the preexisting work that has been recast, transformed, or adapted. Examples of preexisting material might be "Grunewald Altarpiece"; or "19th century quilt design." Do not complete this space for compilations.

Material Added to This Work (space 6b): Give a brief, general statement of the **additional** new material covered by the copyright claim for which registration is sought. In the case of a derivative work, identify this new material. Examples: "Adaptation of design and additional artistic work"; "Reproduction of painting by photolithography"; "Additional cartographic material"; "Compilation of photographs." If the work is a compilation, give a brief, general statement describing both the material that has been compiled **and** the compilation itself. Example: "Compilation of 19th Century Political Cartoons."

7,8,9 SPACE 7, 8, 9: Fee, Correspondence, Certification, Return Address

Deposit Account: If you maintain a Deposit Account in the Copyright Office, identify it in space 7. Otherwise leave the space blank and send the fee of $10 with your application and deposit.

Correspondence (space 7): This space should contain the name, address, area code, and telephone number of the person to be consulted if correspondence about this application becomes necessary.

Certification (space 8): The application cannot be accepted unless it bears the date and the **handwritten signature** of the author or other copyright claimant, or of the owner of exclusive right(s), or of the duly authorized agent of the author, claimant, or owner of exclusive right(s).

Address for Return of Certificate (space 9): The address box must be completed legibly since the certificate will be returned in a window envelope.

MORE INFORMATION

Form of Deposit for Works of the Visual Arts

Exceptions to General Deposit Requirements: As explained on the reverse side of this page, the statutory deposit requirements (generally one copy for unpublished works and two copies for published works) will vary for particular kinds of works of the visual arts. The copyright law authorizes the Register of Copyrights to issue regulations specifying "the administrative classes into which works are to be placed for purposes of deposit and registration, and the nature of the copies or phonorecords to be deposited in the various classes specified." For particular classes, the regulations may require or permit "the deposit of identifying material instead of copies or phonorecords," or "the deposit of only one copy or phonorecord where two would normally be required."

What Should You Deposit? The detailed requirements with respect to the kind of deposit to accompany an application on Form VA are contained in the Copyright

Office Regulations. The following does not cover all of the deposit requirements, but is intended to give you some general guidance.

For an Unpublished Work, the material deposited should represent the entire copyrightable content of the work for which registration is being sought.

For a Published Work, the material deposited should generally consist of two complete copies of the best edition. Exceptions: (1) For certain types of works, one complete copy may be deposited instead of two. These include greeting cards, postcards, stationery, labels, advertisements, scientific drawings, and globes; (2) For most three-dimensional sculptural works, and for certain two-dimensional works, the Copyright Office Regulations require deposit of identifying material (photographs or drawings in a specified form) rather than copies; and (3) Under certain circumstances, for works published in five copies or less or in limited, numbered editions, the deposit may consist of one copy or of identifying reproductions.

FORM VA
UNITED STATES COPYRIGHT OFFICE

REGISTRATION NUMBER

VA   VAU

EFFECTIVE DATE OF REGISTRATION

Month   Day   Year

DO NOT WRITE ABOVE THIS LINE. IF YOU NEED MORE SPACE, USE A SEPARATE CONTINUATION SHEET.

1

TITLE OF THIS WORK ▼

NATURE OF THIS WORK ▼ See instructions

PREVIOUS OR ALTERNATIVE TITLES ▼

PUBLICATION AS A CONTRIBUTION If this work was published as a contribution to a periodical, serial, or collection, give information about the collective work in which the contribution appeared. **Title of Collective Work ▼**

If published in a periodical or serial give: **Volume ▼**   **Number ▼**   **Issue Date ▼**   **On Pages ▼**

2

a
NAME OF AUTHOR ▼

DATES OF BIRTH AND DEATH
Year Born ▼   Year Died ▼

Was this contribution to the work a "work made for hire"?
☐ Yes
☐ No

AUTHOR'S NATIONALITY OR DOMICILE
Name of Country
OR { Citizen of ▶_____
Domiciled in ▶_____

WAS THIS AUTHOR'S CONTRIBUTION TO THE WORK
Anonymous? ☐ Yes ☐ No
Pseudonymous? ☐ Yes ☐ No

If the answer to either of these questions is "Yes," see detailed instructions.

NATURE OF AUTHORSHIP Briefly describe nature of the material created by this author in which copyright is claimed. ▼

NOTE
Under the law, the "author" of a "work made for hire" is generally the employer, not the employee (see instructions). For any part of this work that was "made for hire" check "Yes" in the space provided, give the employer (or other person for whom the work was prepared) as "Author" of that part, and leave the space for dates of birth and death blank.

b
NAME OF AUTHOR ▼

DATES OF BIRTH AND DEATH
Year Born ▼   Year Died ▼

Was this contribution to the work a "work made for hire"?
☐ Yes
☐ No

AUTHOR'S NATIONALITY OR DOMICILE
Name of country
OR { Citizen of ▶_____
Domiciled in ▶_____

WAS THIS AUTHOR'S CONTRIBUTION TO THE WORK
Anonymous? ☐ Yes ☐ No
Pseudonymous? ☐ Yes ☐ No

If the answer to either of these questions is "Yes," see detailed instructions.

NATURE OF AUTHORSHIP Briefly describe nature of the material created by this author in which copyright is claimed. ▼

c
NAME OF AUTHOR ▼

DATES OF BIRTH AND DEATH
Year Born ▼   Year Died ▼

Was this contribution to the work a "work made for hire"?
☐ Yes
☐ No

AUTHOR'S NATIONALITY OR DOMICILE
Name of Country
OR { Citizen of ▶_____
Domiciled in ▶_____

WAS THIS AUTHOR'S CONTRIBUTION TO THE WORK
Anonymous? ☐ Yes ☐ No
Pseudonymous? ☐ Yes ☐ No

If the answer to either of these questions is "Yes," see detailed instructions.

NATURE OF AUTHORSHIP Briefly describe nature of the material created by this author in which copyright is claimed. ▼

3

a
YEAR IN WHICH CREATION OF THIS WORK WAS COMPLETED This information must be given in all cases. ◀ Year

b
DATE AND NATION OF FIRST PUBLICATION OF THIS PARTICULAR WORK
Complete this information ONLY if this work has been published.
Month ▶_____ Day ▶_____ Year ▶_____ ◀ Nation

4

COPYRIGHT CLAIMANT(S) Name and address must be given even if the claimant is the same as the author given in space 2.▼

See instructions before completing this space.

TRANSFER If the claimant(s) named here in space 4 are different from the author(s) named in space 2, give a brief statement of how the claimant(s) obtained ownership of the copyright.▼

DO NOT WRITE HERE OFFICE USE ONLY

APPLICATION RECEIVED

ONE DEPOSIT RECEIVED

TWO DEPOSITS RECEIVED

REMITTANCE NUMBER AND DATE

MORE ON BACK ▶ • Complete all applicable spaces (numbers 5-9) on the reverse side of this page.
• See detailed instructions. • Sign the form at line 8.

DO NOT WRITE HERE

Page 1 of_____pages

EXAMINED BY

CHECKED BY

☐ CORRESPONDENCE
   Yes

FORM VA

FOR
COPYRIGHT
OFFICE
USE
ONLY

DO NOT WRITE ABOVE THIS LINE. IF YOU NEED MORE SPACE, USE A SEPARATE CONTINUATION SHEET.

PREVIOUS REGISTRATION Has registration for this work, or for an earlier version of this work, already been made in the Copyright Office?

☐ **Yes** ☐ **No** If your answer is "Yes," why is another registration being sought? (Check appropriate box) ▼

☐ This is the first published edition of a work previously registered in unpublished form.

☐ This is the first application submitted by this author as copyright claimant.

☐ This is a changed version of the work, as shown by space 6 on this application.

If your answer is "Yes," give: **Previous Registration Number** ▼   **Year of Registration** ▼

5

DERIVATIVE WORK OR COMPILATION Complete both space 6a & 6b for a derivative work; complete only 6b for a compilation.

a. Preexisting Material Identify any preexisting work or works that this work is based on or incorporates. ▼

b. Material Added to This Work Give a brief, general statement of the material that has been added to this work and in which copyright is claimed. ▼

6

See instructions
before completing
this space

DEPOSIT ACCOUNT If the registration fee is to be charged to a Deposit Account established in the Copyright Office, give name and number of Account.

Name ▼   **Account Number** ▼

7

CORRESPONDENCE Give name and address to which correspondence about this application should be sent.   Name/Address/Apt/City/State/Zip ▼

Area Code & Telephone Number ▶

Be sure to
give your
daytime phone
◀ number

CERTIFICATION* I, the undersigned, hereby certify that I am the

Check only one ▼

☐ author

☐ other copyright claimant

☐ owner of exclusive right(s)

☐ authorized agent of_____
                          Name of author or other copyright claimant, or owner of exclusive right(s) ▲

8

of the work identified in this application and that the statements made
by me in this application are correct to the best of my knowledge.

Typed or printed name and date ▼ If this application gives a date of publication in space 3, do not sign and submit it before that date.

_____ **date** ▶ _____

☞ Handwritten signature (X) ▼

**MAIL
CERTIFI-
CATE TO**

Name ▼

Number/Street/Apartment Number ▼

City/State/ZIP ▼

**Certificate
will be
mailed in
window
envelope**

YOU MUST:
• Complete all necessary spaces
• Sign your application in space 8
**SEND ALL 3 ELEMENTS
IN THE SAME PACKAGE:**
1. Application form
2. Non-refundable $10 filing fee
   in check or money order
   payable to *Register of Copyrights*
3. Deposit material
MAIL TO:
Register of Copyrights
Library of Congress
Washington, D.C. 20559

9

* 17 U.S.C. § 506(e) Any person who knowingly makes a false representation of a material fact in the application for copyright registration provided for by section 409, or in any written statement filed in connection with the application, shall be fined not more than $2,500.

June 1989—100,000   U.S. GOVERNMENT PRINTING OFFICE: 1989—241-428 80,023

THE FORMS

TEAR-OUT SECTION

Forms Available on Computer Disk

For ease of modification, the forms may be purchased on computer disk
in PageMaker format for IBM and compatibles, and for the Macintosh.

For further information, please write
Allworth Press, 10 East 23rd Street, New York, NY 10010

❏ **Estimate Form for Client**   ❏ **Preliminary Budget and Schedule**   ❏ **Budget and Schedule Review**

Client_____   Date _____

Project_____   Project No._____

SCOPE OF WORK	TIME			MONEY		
	Allocated	Used	Balance	Budget	Spent	Balance
Design Development _____						
Client Meeting						
Concept Planning						
Preliminary Sketches						
Copywriting						
Art Direction						
Illustration						
Photography						
Comprehensive Layouts						
Changes						
Subtotal						
Mechanical Production _____						
Typography						
Typography (in-house)						
Hand Lettering						
Graphs and Charts						
Technical Renderings						
Photoprocesses						
Line Art						
Photoprints						
Color Stats						
Color Keys						
Retouching						
Photostats (in-house)						
Photocopying						
Other						
Proofreading						
Finished Mechanical Boards						
Changes						
Separations						
Bluelines						
Corrections						
Printing						
Printing Supervision						
Fabrication						
Installation						
Subtotal						
Miscellaneous _____						
Research Materials						
Stylist						
Models						
Travel						
Local Messengers						
Courier Services						
Toll Calls and Fax						
Subtotal						
Total						

This is **not** a contract. The information provided is solely for estimating purposes. Fees, expenses, and time schedules are minimum expected amounts only.

By_____

Proposal Form

Client_____   Date_____

Project_____   By _____

Project Description _____

_____

_____

_____

_____

Scope of Work	Schedule	Fees

1. Concept Planning_____   _____   _____

_____   _____   _____

_____   _____   _____

_____   _____   _____

2. Design Development _____   _____   _____

_____   _____   _____

_____   _____   _____

_____   _____   _____

3. Mechanical Production_____   _____   _____

_____   _____   _____

_____   _____   _____

_____   _____   _____

Expenses Policy	Schedule of Payment

Reimbursables with _____% mark up: _____

_____

_____

Reimbursables at cost: Termination Fee: _____

All information in this proposal is subject to the terms printed on reverse side.

If these terms and rates meet with your approval and we may begin work, please sign below and return a copy to this office.

_____   Date_____

Company Name

_____

Authorized Signature

Terms

1. Fee quoted includes _____ preliminary sketches; additional sketches are $_____ each.

2. Fee quoted includes one set of finished camera-ready mechanicals; changes necessitated by client revisions and/or additions following approvals at each stage (sketches, layout, comps, mechanicals), other than for Designer's error, are billed additionally at $_____ per hour.

3. Rights: All rights to the use of the mechanical boards transfer to the Client, except as noted: _____.

4. Ownership of mechanical boards transfers to client upon full payment of all fees and costs.

5. All invoices are net due within _____ days.

6. Credit: Unless otherwise agreed, Designer shall be accorded a credit line on all printed material, to read as follows:_____

7. Fees quoted are based on work performed during the course of regular working hours (based on a _____ hour week). Overtime, rush, holiday, and weekend work necessitated by Client's directive is billed in addition to the fees quoted.

8. All fees and costs are estimated. Changes in scope of work and/or project specifications require a revision of the information provided on reverse.

9. The information contained in this proposal is valid for thirty days. Proposals approved and signed by the Client are binding upon the Designer and Client commencing on the date of the Client's signature.

10. The Designer's ability to meet deadlines is predicated upon the Client's provision of all necessary information and approvals in a timely manner.

Credit Reference Form

Company Name_____

Address_____

Lenth of time in business:_____

Date_____

Telephone_____

Contact_____

Credit Agencies (Name & Address)	**Telephone No.**	**Account No.**	**Notes**
1		
2		
3		

Banks (Name & Address)	**Telephone No.**	**Account No.**	**Notes**
1		
2		
3		

Trade (Name & Address)	**Telephone No.**	**Contact**
1	
2	
3	

Personal (Name & Address)	**Telephone No.**	**Notes**
1	
2	
3	

By the signature below, authorization and permission is granted to contact the references listed above for the purpose of verifying available credit information on the company and/or individual named above.

_____
Company Name

By:_____
Authorized Signature

Date_____

Jobs Master Index

Date	Client	Job Name	Designer	Invoice #	Job #

Job Sheet

COSTS

Date	Item	Description	Hrs/Rate	Total

INFORMATION

Job

Client

Address

Contact

Telephone

Bill To

Ship To

P.O. #

DATES

Job In _____ Sketch Due _____

Finish Due _____ Other _____ Accepted _____

BILLING

Fee _____ ☐ Time ☐ Costs State Tax _____ %

Inv # _____

Date _____

Amt _____

Inv # _____

Date _____

Amt _____

Job Number

DESCRIPTION OF JOB

Source _____

BIDDING ESTIMATES

Date	Item	Vendor	Amt	Accepted

WORK CHANGE ORDERS

Date	Item		Ordered By

SUMMARY OF COSTS

Item	Est	Actual	M/U	Billed
Fee				
Meetings				
Design Development				
Comps				
Mechanicals				
AA's				
Extras				
Art Direction				
Printing Supervision				
Travel				
Typography				
Line Art (Stats)				
Photo Prints				
Retouching				
In-House Stats				
In-House Photocopies				
Illustration				
Photography				
Stylist				
Other Talent				
Printing				
Fabrication				
Local Messengers				
Courier Services				
Toll Calls & Fax				
Tax				
Totals				
Profit				

COSTS

Date	Item	Description	Hrs/Rate	Total

COSTS

Date	Item	Description	Hrs/Rate	Total

Job Number

Time Sheet

Name _____

Dates _____

Month _____

Year _____

Job#	Job Name	Job Phase	Activity	Mon Reg/OT	Tue Reg/OT	Wed Reg/OT	Thu Reg/OT	Fri Reg/OT	Total Reg/OT	Ok to Bill	Posted

Nonbillables

	Mon	Tue	Wed	Thu	Fri	Total
Administration						
Clean-up						
Promotion						
Holidays						
Sick Days						
Other (explain)						
Totals						

Approved _____

Studio Production Schedule

Client _____

Job Name _____

Job Number _____

Date _____

Item	Dates	Due Dates	To/From	Delivered
Preliminary Meetings				
Materials Due (Specs/Copy)				
Sketch Presentation				
Client Approval				
Design Development				
Layouts/Comps				
Client Approval				
Art Direction				
Photography				
Illustration				
Other (Copywriting)				
Type Specifications				
Mechanicals				
Client Approval				
Revisions/Corrections				
Separations				
Printing				
Fabrication/Installation				
Delivery				

Project Status Report

To _____

Copies _____

Project Number _____

Project Title _____

Date _____

Phase	Item	Status	Next Action	Date Due
Preliminaries				
Design Development				
Art Direction				
Layouts				
Mechanicals				
Printing/Fabrication				
Other				

Work Change Order

Client _____   Date_____

Project_____   Project No._____

Work Change Requested By_____

Stage of work   Sketches _____

                             Comps _____

                            Layout _____

                     Mechanicals _____

                       Bluelines _____

          Printing/Fabrication _____

                    Typesetting _____

                 Art Direction _____

                Other (explain) _____

Content Change   Conceptual _____

                             Copy _____

                      Illustration _____

                   Photography _____

Specifications Change   Typography _____

                           Colors _____

                             Size _____

                     Pagination _____

                  Reproduction _____

                        Shipping _____

                Other (explain) _____

Remarks_____

_____

_____

_____

_____

This is not an invoice. Revised specifications on work in progress represents information that is different from what the designer based the original project proposal. The following estimated charges in time and cost are approximate.

          Estimated Additional Time_____

          Estimated Additional Cost_____

Kindly sign and return a copy of this form. The information contained in this work change order is assumed to be correct and acceptable to the client unless the designer is otherwise notified in writing within_____ days of the date of this document.

          Approved by_____   Date_____

Estimate Request Form

Client _____   Date _____

Project _____   Project No. _____

Request By _____   Telephone _____

To _____

_____

_____

SPECIFICATIONS/DESCRIPTION		
Quantity	**Item**	**Estimate**
_____	_____	_____
_____	_____	_____
_____	_____	_____
_____	_____	_____
_____	_____	_____
_____	_____	_____
_____	_____	_____
_____	_____	_____
_____	_____	_____
_____	_____	_____
_____	_____	_____
_____	_____	_____
_____	_____	_____
_____	_____	_____

Delivery Date _____

Subtotal _____

Tax _____

SPECIAL NOTES

Shipping/Delivery _____

_____

Total _____

_____

_____

Deposit Required _____

_____

Quotation by _____   Date _____

This is not a purchase order. The information contained in this form is to provide a basis for estimating the cost of the services requested.
It is understood that the estimated costs are approximate and that final billing will be adjusted according to specific instructions provided
in a purchase order or contract.
Kindly fill in the information requested in the shaded area under Estimate, sign, date, and return a copy of this form by _____
Thank you.

Purchase Order

Number

Client_____ Date_____

Project_____ Project No._____

To_____

_____

_____

Schedule: Date Required _____   ❑ Regular   ❑ Rush   ❑ O.T.

Specifications: _____

_____

_____

_____

_____

_____

_____

_____

_____

_____

_____

_____

_____

_____

Ship to_____   Subtotal _____

_____   Tax _____

_____   Shipping _____

_____   Total _____

Bill to_____

_____

_____

_____

Ordered by_____   Tel._____ Ext._____

Requisition Form

Name _____

Telephone Extension _____   Date _____

Delivery
❑ Regular
❑ Rush

Source Codes

1. Catalogue (Include name of catalogue, page number, item number, brief description, quantities, and unit prices)
2. Internal Supplies (Include name of item, description including sizes and colors, and quantities)
3. Other (Include name of source, address and telephone number, a description of the item including sizes, colors, quantities, and unit price)

Source Code	Description	Unit Price	Job Number

Payables Index

Date Received	Company/OL Name	Amount	Invoice #	Date	Attention	Approved

Transmittal Form

To_____ From_____

Company_____ Date_____

Project_____ Project Number_____

Copies to_____

For ━━

❑ Review   ❑ Files   ❑ Information
❑ Approval   ❑ Distribution   ❑ As Requested

Via ━━

❑ Fax (Number of pages, including transmittal_____)
❑ Messenger   ❑ UPS   ❑ Inter-Office
❑ Courier Service (_____)
❑ US Mail (regular)   ❑ US Mail (express)
❑ Freight Forwarder (_____)

Enclosed ━━

❑ Artwork   ❑ Comps   ❑ Mechanicals
❑ Photographs   ❑ Color Xeroxes   ❑ Transparencies
❑ Blueprints   ❑ Sepias   ❑ Mylars
❑ Typeset Copy   ❑ Samples   ❑ Model
❑ Article   ❑ Book   ❑ Promotion Package
❑ Other (_____)

Disposition ━━

❑ Kindly Reply   ❑ Return   ❑ Keep   ❑ Distribute

Remarks_____

_____

_____

_____

_____

_____

_____

_____

_____

_____

_____

_____

_____

Artwork Log

Date	Time	Job #	To	Description	Via	Due Back	Returned	Location

Billing Index

Date	Invoice #	Job #	Billed To	Job Name	Fee	Production	Tax	Total	Paid

Invoice

Date _____

Invoice Number _____

Project Number _____

To _____

_____

_____

_____

Attention _____   Purchase Order No._____

Project Title_____

Description of Services	Fees/Costs
_____	_____
_____	_____
_____	_____
_____	_____
_____	_____
_____	_____
_____	_____
_____	_____
_____	_____
_____	_____
_____	_____

Subtotal _____

Tax _____

Total _____

Terms: Kindly remit amount due net _____ days.

All original artwork remains the property of the artist, except as noted:_____

_____

Rights transferred are limited to:_____

❏ All other rights reserved.

❏ Rights specified herein and ownership of mechanical boards transfer to client upon full payment of all fees and costs.

Invoice

Date _____

Invoice Number _____

Project Number _____

To _____

_____

_____

_____

Attention _____ Purchase Order No._____

Project Title _____

Design Development
- ❏ Client Meetings
- ❏ Concept Planning
- ❏ Preliminary Sketches
- ❏ Copywriting
- ❏ Art Direction
- ❏ Comprehensive Layouts
- ❏ Photography
- ❏ Illustration
- ❏ Changes

_____

_____

_____

_____

Design Subtotal _____

Mechanical Production and Reimbursable Expenses

	Rate	Total		Rate	Total
Type Specifications	_____	_____	Proofreading	_____	_____
Typography (out)	_____	_____	Finished Mechanicals	_____	_____
Typography (in)	_____	_____	Changes	_____	_____
AA's	_____	_____	Separations	_____	_____
Hand Lettering	_____	_____	Printing	_____	_____
Graphs and Charts	_____	_____	Printing Supervision	_____	_____
Technical Rendering	_____	_____	Fabrication	_____	_____
Line Art	_____	_____	Installation	_____	_____
Photoprints	_____	_____	Research Materials	_____	_____
Color stats	_____	_____	Stylist	_____	_____
Color Keys	_____	_____	Models	_____	_____
Photoprocessing	_____	_____	Travel	_____	_____
Retouching	_____	_____	Local Messengers	_____	_____
Stats (out)	_____	_____	Courier Services	_____	_____
Stats (in)	_____	_____	Freight	_____	_____
Photocopying	_____	_____	Toll Calls & Fax	_____	_____
Other_____	_____	_____	Production Subtotal (2)		_____
Production Subtotal (1)		_____	Subtotal		_____
			Tax		_____
			Total		_____

See reverse side for terms of agreement.

Terms

Kindly remit amount due net _____ days.

All original artwork remains the property of the artist, except as noted:

_____

_____

_____

_____

_____

Rights transferred are limited to:

_____

_____

_____

_____

❏ All other rights reserved.

Credit line to read as follows:

_____

_____

_____

Rights specified herein and ownership of mechanical boards transfer to client upon full payment of all fees and costs.

Statement

Date _____

To_____
_____
_____
_____

Attention_____

Reference_____
_____
_____

Please be advised that payment for the following has not been received as of today's date.

Date of Invoice	Invoice Number	Amount Due
_____	_____	_____
_____	_____	_____
_____	_____	_____
_____	_____	_____
_____	_____	_____
_____	_____	_____
_____	_____	_____
_____	_____	_____
_____	_____	_____
_____	_____	_____

We would greatly appreciate your prompt attention and earliest payment possible. Please call if you have any questions or comments about this statement.

Call_____   Telephone Number_____

Signature_____

Second Notice

Date _____

To_____

_____

_____

_____

Attention _____

Reference_____

_____

_____

Statement Date	Date of Invoice	Invoice Number	Amount Due
_____	_____	_____	_____
_____	_____	_____	_____
_____	_____	_____	_____
_____	_____	_____	_____

Sorry not to have heard from you. This is the second time we have had to contact you about this overdue account.

If you cannot make immediate payment in the full amount, please call right away.

Call_____ Telephone Number_____

Signature_____

Final Notice

Date _____

To_____

_____

_____

_____

Attention_____

Reference_____

_____

_____

This account is now seriously in arrears. We have repeatedly requested payment and have neither received payment nor have we been contacted with an explanation.

We must collect immediately, and, if we are not satisfied within ten days, we have no choice but to turn this account over for collection. Be aware that this process may result in additional legal and court costs to you and may damage your credit rating.

It is not too late to contact us.

Call_____ Telephone Number_____

Signature_____

Project Confirmation Agreement

AGREEMENT as of the _____ day of _____, 19 _____, between _____, located at _____ (hereinafter referred to as the "Client") and _____, located at _____ (hereinafter referred to as the "Designer") with respect to the creation of a certain design or designs (hereinafter referred to as the "Designs").

WHEREAS, Designer is a professional designer of good standing;

WHEREAS, Client wishes the Designer to create certain Designs described more fully herein; and

WHEREAS, Designer wishes to create such Designs;

NOW, THEREFORE, in consideration of the foregoing premises and the mutual covenants hereinafter set forth and other valuable considerations, the parties hereto agree as follows:

1. Description. The Designer agrees to create the Designs in accordance with the following specifications:

Project description_____

Number of finished designs_____

Other specifications_____

The Designs shall be delivered in the form of one set of finished camera-ready mechanicals, unless specified to the contrary here_____

Other services to be rendered by Designer_____

_____

Client purchase order number_____Job number_____

2. Due Date. The Designer agrees to deliver sketches within _____ days after the later of the signing of this Agreement or, if the Client is to provide reference, layouts, or specifications, after the Client has provided same to the Designer. The Designs shall be delivered _____ days after the approval of sketches by the Client.

3. Grant of Rights. Upon receipt of full payment, Designer grants to the Client the following rights in the Designs:

For use as_____

For the product or publication named_____

In the following territory_____

For the following time period_____

Other limitations_____

With respect to the usage shown above, the Client shall have ❏ exclusive ❏ nonexclusive rights.

4. Reservation of Rights. All rights not expressly granted hereunder are reserved to the Designer, including but not limited to all rights in sketches, comps, or other preliminary materials created by the Designer.

5. Fee. Client agrees to pay the following purchase price: $_____ for the usage rights granted. Client agrees to pay sales tax, if required.

6. Additional Usage. If Client wishes to make any additional uses of the Designs, Client agrees to seek permission from the Designer and make such payments as are agreed to between the parties at that time.

7. Expenses. Client agrees to reimburse the Designer for all expenses of production as well as related expenses including but not limited to illustration, photography, travel, models, props, messengers, and telephone. These expenses shall be marked up _____ percent by the Designer when billed to the Client.

At the time of signing this Agreement, Client shall pay Designer $_____ as a nonrefundable advance against expenses. If the advance exceeds expenses incurred, the credit balance shall be used to reduce the fee payable or, if the fee has been fully paid, shall be reimbursed to Client.

8. Payment. Client agrees to pay the Designer within thirty days of the date of Designer's billing, which shall be dated as of the date of delivery of the Designs. In the event that work is postponed at the request of the Client, the Designer shall have the right to bill pro rata for work completed through the date of that request, while reserving all other rights under this Agreement. Overdue payments shall be subject to interest charges of _____ percent monthly.

9. **Advances.** At the time of signing this Agreement, Client shall pay Designer ____ percent of the fee as an advance against the total fee. Upon approval of sketches Client shall pay Designer ____ percent of the fee as an advance against the total fee.

10. **Revisions.** The Designer shall be given the first opportunity to make any revisions requested by the Client. If the revisions are not due to any fault on the part of the Designer, an additional fee shall be charged. If the Designer objects to any revisions to be made by the Client, the Designer shall have the right to have his or her name removed from the published Designs.

11. **Copyright Notice.** Copyright notice in the name of the Designer ❑ shall ❑ shall not accompany the Designs when reproduced.

12. **Authorship Credit.** Authorship credit in the name of the Designer ❑ shall ❑ shall not accompany the Designs when reproduced.

13. **Cancellation.** In the event of cancellation by the Client, the following cancellation payment shall be paid by the Client: **(A)** Cancellation prior to the Designs being turned in: ____ percent of the fee; **(B)** Cancellation due to the Designs being unsatisfactory: ____ percent of fee; and **(C)** Cancellation for any other reason after the Designs are turned in: ____ percent of fee. In the event of cancellation, the Designer shall own all rights in the Designs. The billing upon cancellation shall be payable within thirty days of the Client's notification to stop work or the delivery of the Designs, whichever occurs sooner.

14. **Ownership and Return of Designs.** Upon Designer's receipt of full payment, the camera-ready mechanicals delivered to the Client shall become the property of the Client. The ownership of original artwork, including but not limited to sketches and any other materials created in the process of making the Designs as well as illustrations or photographic materials such as transparencies, shall remain with the Designer and, if delivered by Designer to Client with the mechanicals, shall be returned to the Designer by bonded messenger, air freight, or registered mail within thirty days of the Client's completing its use of the mechanicals. The parties agree that the value of original design, art, or photography is $_____, and these originals are described as follows _____

15. **Releases.** The Client agrees to indemnify and hold harmless the Designer against any and all claims, costs, and expenses, including attorney's fees, due to materials included in the Designs at the request of the Client for which no copyright permission or privacy release was requested or uses which exceed the uses allowed pursuant to a permission or release.

16. **Arbitration.** All disputes arising under this Agreement shall be submitted to binding arbitration before _____ in the following location _____ and settled in accordance with the rules of the American Arbitration Association. Judgment upon the arbitration award may be entered in any court having jurisdiction thereof. Disputes in which the amount at issue is less than $_____ shall not be subject to this arbitration provision.

17. **Miscellany.** This Agreement shall be binding upon the parties hereto, their heirs, successors, assigns, and personal representatives. This Agreement constitutes the entire understanding between the parties. Its terms can be modified only by an instrument in writing signed by both parties, except that the Client may authorize expenses or revisions orally. A waiver of a breach of any of the provisions of this Agreement shall not be construed as a continuing waiver of other breaches of the same or other provisions hereof. This Agreement shall be governed by the laws of the State of _____.

IN WITNESS WHEREOF, the parties hereto have signed this Agreement as of the date first set forth above.

Designer_____   Client_____
                        Company Name   Company Name

By_____   By_____
                Authorized Signatory, Title   Authorized Signatory, Title

Contract with Illustrator or Photographer

AGREEMENT entered into as of the _____ day of _____, 19 _____, between _____, located at _____ (hereinafter referred to as the "Supplier") and_____, located at _____ (hereinafter referred to as the "Designer") with respect to the creation of certain images (hereinafter referred to as the "Images").

WHEREAS, Supplier is a professional illustrator or photographer of good standing;

WHEREAS, Designer wishes the Supplier to create the Images described more fully herein; and

WHEREAS, Supplier wishes to create such Images pursuant to this Agreement;

NOW, THEREFORE, in consideration of the foregoing premises and the mutual covenants hereinafter set forth and other valuable considerations, the parties hereto agree as follows:

1. **Description.** The Supplier agrees to create the Images in accordance with the following specifications:
    Project title and description of Images _____
    _____
    _____
    Other specifications _____
    _____
    Other services to be rendered by Supplier _____
    _____

2. **Due Date.** The Supplier agrees to deliver the Images within _____ days after the later of the signing of this Agreement or, if the Designer is to provide reference, layouts, or specifications, after the Designer has provided same to the Supplier. If the Designer is to review and approve the work in progress, specify the details here _____

3. **Grant of Rights.** Supplier hereby grants to the Designer the following exclusive rights to use the Images:
    For use as_____
    For the product or publication named_____
    These rights shall be worldwide and for the full life of the copyright and any renewals thereof unless specified to the contrary here_____

4. **Fee.** Designer agrees to pay the following purchase price: $_____ for the usage rights granted. If the fee is variable, it shall be computed as follows_____
    _____

5. **Expenses.** Designer agrees to reimburse the Supplier for expenses incurred in creating the Images, provided that such expenses shall be itemized and supported by invoices, shall not be marked up, and shall not exceed $_____ in total.

6. **Payment.** Designer agrees to pay the Supplier within thirty days of the date of Supplier's billing, which shall be dated as of the date of delivery of the Images. In the event that work is postponed or cancelled at the request of the Designer, the Supplier shall have the right to bill and be paid pro rata for work completed through the date of that request, but the Designer shall have no further liability hereunder.

7. **Revisions or Reshoots.** The Supplier shall be given the first opportunity to make any revisions or reshoots requested by the Designer. If the revisions or reshoots are not due to any fault on the part of the Supplier, an additional fee shall be charged as follows _____.
    If the Supplier objects to any revisions to be made by the Designer, the Supplier shall have the right to have any authorship credit and copyright notice in his or her name removed from the Images.

8. Authorship Credit. Authorship credit in the name of the Supplier ❑ shall ❑ shall not accompany the Images when reproduced.

9. Copyright Notice. Copyright notice in the name of the Supplier ❑ shall ❑ shall not accompany the Images when reproduced.

10. Ownership of Physical Images. The ownership of the physical Images in the form delivered shall be the property of _____. Sketches and any other materials created in the process of making the finished Images shall remain the property of the Supplier, unless indicated to the contrary here _____

11. Releases. The Supplier agrees to obtain releases for any art, photography, or other copyrighted materials to be incorporated by the Supplier into the Images.

12. Warranty and Indemnity. The Supplier warrants and represents that he or she is the sole creator of the Images and owns all rights granted under this Agreement, that the Images are an original creation (except for materials obtained with the written permission of others or materials from the public domain), that the Images do not infringe any other person's copyrights or rights of literary property, nor do they violate the rights of privacy of, or libel, other persons. The Supplier agrees to indemnify and hold harmless the Designer against any claims, judgments, court costs, attorney's fees, and other expenses arising from any alleged or actual breach of this warranty.

13. Arbitration. All disputes arising under this Agreement shall be submitted to binding arbitration before_____ _____ in the following location _____ and settled in accordance with the rules of the American Arbitration Association. Judgment upon the arbitration award may be entered in any court having jurisdiction thereof. Disputes in which the amount at issue is less than $_____ shall not be subject to this arbitration provision.

14. Assignment. The Designer shall have the right to assign any or all of its rights and obligations pursuant to this Agreement. The Supplier shall have the right to assign monies due to him or her under the terms of this Agreement, but shall not make any other assignments hereunder.

15. Term and Termination. This Agreement shall have a term ending _____ months after payment pursuant to Paragraph 6. The Designer may terminate this Agreement at any time prior to the Supplier's commencement of work and may terminate thereafter if the Supplier fails to adhere to the specifications or schedule for the Images. This Agreement shall also terminate in the event of the Supplier's bankruptcy or insolvency. The rights and obligations of the parties pursuant to Paragraphs 3, 8, 9, 10, 11, 12, 13, and 14 shall survive termination of this Agreement.

16. Miscellany. This Agreement constitutes the entire understanding between the parties. Its terms can be modified only by an instrument in writing signed by both parties. A waiver of a breach of any of the provisions of this Agreement shall not be construed as a continuing waiver of other breaches of the same or other provisions hereof. This Agreement shall be binding upon the parties hereto and their respective heirs, successors, assigns, and personal representatives. This Agreement shall be governed by the laws of the State of _____.

IN WITNESS WHEREOF, the parties hereto have signed this Agreement as of the date first set forth above.

Supplier _____   Designer _____
                                                                          Company Name

                                                              By _____
                                                                          Authorized Signatory, Title

Contract with Printer

AGREEMENT entered into as of the _____ day of _____ 19____, between _____ (hereinafter referred to as the "Designer"), located at _____, and _____ (hereinafter referred to as the "Printer"), located at _____ , with respect to the printing of certain materials (hereinafter referred to as the "Work").

WHEREAS, the Designer has prepared the Work for publication and wishes to have the Work printed in accordance with the terms of this Agreement; and

WHEREAS, the Printer is in the business of printing and is prepared to meet the specifications and other terms of this Agreement with respect to printing the Work;

NOW, THEREFORE, in consideration of the foregoing premises and the mutual covenants hereinafter set forth and other valuable consideration, the parties hereto agree as follows:

1. **Specifications.** The Printer agrees to print the Work in accordance with ❏ Schedule A or ❏ the following specifications:

   Title_____

   Description_____

   _____

   _____

   Quantity_____

   Repro Materials_____

   _____

   _____

   Stock_____

   PrePress_____

   Proofs_____

   Binding_____

   Packing_____

   Other specifications_____

   _____

2. **Delivery and Risk of Loss.** Printer agrees to deliver the order on or before _____, 19_____ to the following location _____ and pursuant to the following terms _____. The Printer shall be strictly liable for loss, damage, or theft of the order until delivery has been made as provided in this paragraph. Time is of the essence with respect to the delivery date.

3. **Price.** The price for the quantity specified in Paragraph 1 shall be $_____. Overs and unders shall not be acceptable unless specified to the contrary here _____, in which case the price shall be adjusted at the rate of $_____ per thousand.

4. **Payment.** The price shall be payable within _____ days of delivery.

5. **Ownership and Return of Supplied Materials.** All camera-ready copy, artwork, film, separations, and any other materials supplied by the Designer to the Printer shall remain the exclusive property of the Designer and be returned by the Printer at its expense as soon as possible upon the earlier of either the printing of the Work or the Designer's request. The Printer shall be liable for any loss or damage to such materials from the time of receipt

until the time of return receipt by the Designer. The Printer ❑ shall ❑ shall not insure such materials for the benefit of the Designer in the amount of $_____.

6. **Ownership and Return of Commissioned Materials.** All materials created by the Printer for the Designer, including but not limited to sketches, copy, dummies, working mechanical art, type, negatives, positives, flats, plates, or belts, shall become the exclusive property of the Designer and shall be stored without expense by the Printer and be returned at the Designer's request. The expense of such return of materials shall be paid by the ❑ Printer ❑ Designer. The Printer shall be liable for any loss or damage to such materials from the time of creation until the time of return receipt by the Designer. The Printer ❑ shall ❑ shall not insure such materials for the benefit of the Designer in the amount of $_____.

7. **Proofs.** If proofs are requested in the specifications, the Work shall not be printed until such proofs have been approved in writing by the Designer. The finished copies of the Work shall match the quality of the proofs.

8. **Arbitration.** All disputes arising under this Agreement shall be submitted to binding arbitration before _____ _____ at the following location _____ and the arbitration award may be entered for judgment in any court having jurisdiction thereof. Notwithstanding the foregoing, either party may refuse to arbitrate when the dispute is for less than $_____.

9. **Term and Termination.** This Agreement shall have a term ending _____ months after payment pursuant to Paragraph 4. The Designer may terminate this Agreement at any time prior to the Printer's commencement of work and may terminate thereafter if the Printer fails to adhere to the specifications or production schedule for the Work. This Agreement shall also terminate in the event of the Printer's bankruptcy or insolvency. The rights and obligations of the parties pursuant to Paragraphs 5, 6, and 8 shall survive termination of the Agreement.

10. **Miscellany.** This Agreement contains the entire understanding between the parties and may not be modified, amended, or changed except by an instrument in writing signed by both parties. A waiver of any breach of any of the provisions of this Agreement shall not be construed as a continuing waiver of other breaches of the same or other provisions hereof. This Agreement shall be binding upon the parties hereto and their respective heirs, successors, assigns, and personal representatives. This Agreement shall be interpreted under the laws of the State of _____.

IN WITNESS WHEREOF, the parties have signed this Agreement as of the date first set forth above.

Printer_____   Designer_____
        Company Name   Company Name

By_____   By_____
   Authorized Signatory, Title   Authorized Signatory, Title

Schedule A ❏ **Request for Printing Quotation**   ❏ **Printing Specifications**

Printer _____   Designer _____

Address _____   Address _____

_____   _____

Contact Person _____   Contact Person _____

Phone _____   Phone _____

Job Name _____   Job Number _____

Description _____   Date for Quotation _____

_____   Date Job to Printer _____

_____   Date Job Needed _____

Quantity: 1) _____ 2) _____ 3) _____ ❏ Additional _____

Size: Flat Trim _____ x _____   Folded/ Bound to _____ x _____

Number of Pages _____   ❏ Self Cover   ❏ Plus Cover   ❏ Cover Bleed

Design includes: ❏ Page Bleeds # _____   ❏ Screen Tints # _____   ❏ Reverses # _____

Halftones Print: ❏ Halftone (black) # _____   ❏ Duotone (black plus PMS _____) # _____

Size of Halftones _____

Color Requirements:

Cover: ❏ 4 Color Process ❏ Spot Colors PMS #s _____ plus Black

Inside: ❏ Full Color   ❏ Spot Color PMS #s _____   ❏ Color Signatures only # _____

Color Separations: ❏ transparencies # _____   ❏ reflective art # _____   ❏ provided by client

Original art will be supplied in a: ❏ scanable form   ❏ rigid form

Sizes of finished separations _____

Coatings: Overall Varnish / Spot Varnish   │   Gloss Varnish / Dull Varnish / Liquid Lamination / UV Coating

Cover   ❏   ❏   │   ❏   ❏   ❏   ❏

Inside   ❏   ❏   │   ❏   ❏   ❏   ❏

Special instructions _____

_____

_____

Mechanicals:

Color breaks shown: ❑ on acetate overlays ❑ on tissues ❑ # of pieces of separate line art _____

Paper Stock: Name   Weight   Grade   Finish   Color

Cover_____   _____   _____   _____   _____

Inside_____   _____   _____   _____   _____

Insert / Other_____   _____   _____   _____   _____

❑ Send samples of paper   ❑ Make book dummy

Other Printing Specifications:

❑ Special Inks _____

❑ Die Cutting ❑ Embossing ❑ Engraving ❑ Foil Stamping ❑ Thermography ❑ Serial Numbering

❑ Other _____

_____

Proofs: ❑ Blues   ❑ Color Keys   ❑ Chromalins   ❑ Progressives   ❑ Press Proofs

Details _____

Bindery: ❑ Hard Bound   ❑ Perfect Bound   ❑ Spiral Bound   ❑ Ring Binder   ❑ Saddle Stitch

❑ Score   ❑ Perforate   ❑ Fold   ❑ Drill   ❑ Punch   ❑ Round Corners   ❑ Tip In

Details _____

Packing: ❑ Rubber/String/Paper Band in #_____   ❑ Shrink Wrap in #_____   ❑ Bulk in Cartons

❑ Maximum weight per carton _____lbs   ❑ Skids   ❑ Pallets   ❑ Other _____

Shipping:

Deliver To _____

_____

_____

❑ Truck   ❑ Rail   ❑ Sea   ❑ Air   ❑ Drop Ship   ❑ UPS/Other _____

❑ Customer pick up   ❑ Separate shipping costs   ❑ Send cheapest way   ❑ Other _____

Shipment terms _____   ❑ Insure for _____ percent of printing cost

Miscellaneous instructions: _____

_____

_____

_____

_____

_____

_____

Designer—Sales Agent Contract

AGREEMENT, entered into as of this _____ day of _____, 19_____, between _____ (hereinafter referred to as the "Designer"), located at _____, and _____ (hereinafter referred to as the "Agent"), located at _____,

WHEREAS, the Designer is an established designer of proven talents; and

WHEREAS, the Designer wishes to have an agent represent him or her in marketing certain rights enumerated herein; and

WHEREAS, the Agent is capable of marketing the work produced by the Designer; and

WHEREAS, the Agent wishes to represent the Designer;

NOW, THEREFORE, in consideration of the foregoing premises and the mutual covenants hereinafter set forth and other valuable consideration, the parties hereto agree as follows:

1. **Agency**. The Designer appoints the Agent to act as his or her representative:

    (A) in the following geographical area _____

    (B) for the following markets:

    ❏ Advertising   ❏ Corporate   ❏ Book Publishing   ❏ Magazines

    ❏ Other, specified as _____

    (C) for the following types of art or design_____

    (D) to be the Designer's ❏ exclusive ❏ nonexclusive agent for the area, markets, and types of work indicated.

    Any rights not granted to the Agent are reserved to the Designer.

2. **Best Efforts.** The Agent agrees to use his or her best efforts in submitting the Designer's work for the purpose of securing assignments for the Designer. The Agent shall negotiate the terms of any assignment that is offered, but the Designer may reject any assignment if he or she finds the terms thereof unacceptable.

3. **Samples.** The Designer shall provide the Agent with such samples of work as are from time to time necessary for the purpose of securing assignments. These samples shall remain the property of the Designer and be returned on termination of this Agreement. The Agent shall take reasonable efforts to protect the work from loss or damage, but shall be liable for such loss or damage only if caused by the Agent's negligence.

4. **Term.** This Agreement shall take effect as of the date first set forth above, and remain in full force and effect for a term of _____, unless terminated as provided in Paragraph 11.

5. **Commissions.** The Agent shall be entitled to the following commissions: **(A)** On assignments obtained by the Agent during the term of this Agreement, _____ percent of the billing. **(B)** On house accounts, _____ percent of the billing. For purposes of this Agreement, house accounts are defined as accounts obtained by the Designer at any time or obtained by another agent representing the Designer prior to the commencement of this Agreement and are listed in the Schedule of House Accounts attached to this Agreement. **(C)** For books which the Designer authors or coauthors, _____ percent of the royalties or licensing proceeds paid to the Designer by the publisher or its licensees.

    It is understood by both parties that no commissions shall be paid on assignments rejected by the Designer or for which the Designer fails to receive payment, regardless of the reason payment is not made. Further, no commissions shall be payable in either **(A)** or **(B)** above for any part of the billing that is due to expenses incurred by the Designer in performing the assignment, whether or not such expenses are reimbursed by the client. In the event that a flat fee is paid by the client, it shall be reduced by the amount of expenses incurred by the Designer in performing the assignment, and the Agent's commission shall be payable only on the fee as reduced for expenses.

6. **Billing.** The ❑ Designer ❑ Agent shall be responsible for all billings.

7. **Payments.** The party responsible for billing shall make all payments due within _____ days of receipt of any fees covered by this Agreement. Such payments due shall be be deemed trust funds and shall not be intermingled with funds belonging to the party responsible for billing and payment. Late payments shall be accompanied by interest calculated at the rate of _____ percent per month thereafter.

8. **Promotional Expenses.** Promotional expenses, including but not limited to promotional mailings and paid advertising, shall be mutually agreed to by the parties and paid _____ percent by the Agent and _____ percent by the Designer. The Agent shall bear the expenses of shipping, insurance, and similar marketing expenses.

9. **Accountings.** The party responsible for billing shall send copies of invoices to the other party when rendered. If requested, that party shall also provide the other party with semiannual accountings showing all assignments for the period, the clients' names and addresses, the fees paid, expenses incurred by the Designer, the dates of payment, the amounts on which the Agent's commissions are to be calculated, and the sums due less those amounts already paid.

10. **Inspection of the Books and Records.** The party responsible for the billing shall keep the books and records with respect to payments due each party at his or her place of business and permit the other party to inspect these books and records during normal business hours on the giving of reasonable notice.

11. **Termination.** This Agreement may be terminated by either party by giving thirty (30) days written notice to the other party. If the Designer receives assignments after the termination date from clients originally obtained by the Agent during the term of this Agreement, the commission specified in Paragraph 5(A) shall be payable to the Agent under the following circumstances. If the Agent has represented the Designer for _____ months or less, the Agent shall receive a commission on such assignments received by the Designer within _____ days of the date of termination. This period shall increase by thirty (30) days for each additional _____ months that the Agent has represented the Designer, but in no event shall such period exceed _____ days. In the event of the bankruptcy or insolvency of the Agent, this Agreement shall also terminate. The rights and obligations under Paragraphs 3, 6, 7, 8, 9, and 10 shall survive termination.

12. **Assignment.** This Agreement shall not be assigned by either of the parties hereto, except that the Designer shall have the right to assign any monies due the Designer under this Agreement.

13. **Arbitration.** Any disputes arising under this Agreement shall be settled by arbitration before _____ under the rules of the American Arbitration Association in the City of _____, except that the parties shall have the right to go to court for claims of $_____ or less. Any award rendered by the arbitrator may be entered in any court having jurisdiction thereof.

14. **Notices.** All notices shall be given to the parties at their respective addresses set forth above.

15. **Independent Contractor Status.** Both parties agree that the Agent is acting as an independent contractor. This Agreement is not an employment agreement, nor does it constitute a joint venture or partnership between the Designer and Agent.

16. **Amendments, Mergers, Successors and Assigns.** All amendments to this Agreement must be written. This Agreement incorporates the entire understanding of the parties. It shall be binding on and inure to the benefit of the successors, administrators, executors, or heirs of the Agent and Designer.

17. **Governing Law.** This Agreement shall be governed by the laws of the State of _____.

IN WITNESS WHEREOF, the parties have signed this Agreement as of the date set forth above.

Designer_____   Agent_____
             Company name   Company name

By_____   By_____
     Authorized Signatory, Title   Authorized Signatory, Title

Schedule of House Accounts

Date_____

1._____

(name and address of client)

2._____

3._____

4._____

5._____

6._____

7._____

8._____

9._____

10._____

11._____

12._____

13._____

14._____

15._____

16._____

17._____

18._____

19._____

20._____

Designer's Lecture Contract

AGREEMENT, dated the _____ day of _____, 19 ____, between_____ (hereinafter referred to as the "Designer"), located at _____and _____(hereinafter referred to as the "Sponsor"), located at _____.

WHEREAS, the Sponsor is familiar with and admires the work of the Designer; and

WHEREAS, the Sponsor wishes the Designer to visit the Sponsor to enhance the opportunities for its students to have contact with working professional designer; and

WHEREAS, the Designer wishes to lecture with respect to his or her work and perform such other services as this contract may call for;

NOW, THEREFORE, in consideration of the foregoing premises and the mutual covenants hereinafter set forth and other valuable considerations, the parties hereto agree as follows:

1. **Designer to Lecture.** The Designer hereby agrees to come to the Sponsor on the following date(s):_____ _____ and perform the following services: _____. The Designer shall use best efforts to make his or her services as productive as possible to the Sponsor. The Designer further agrees to bring examples of his or her own work in the form of _____ _____.

2. **Payment.** The Sponsor agrees to pay as full compensation for the Designer's services rendered under Paragraph 1 the sum of $_____. This sum shall be payable to the Designer on completion of the _____ day of the Designer's residence with the Sponsor.

3. **Expenses.** In addition to the payments provided under Paragraph 2, the Sponsor agrees to reimburse the Designer for the following expenses:

   (A) Travel expenses in the amount of $_____.

   (B) Food and lodging expenses in the amount of $_____.

   (C) Other expenses listed here:_____in the amount of $_____.

   The reimbursement for travel expenses shall be made fourteen (14) days prior to the earliest date specified in Paragraph 1. The reimbursement for food, lodging, and other expenses shall be made at the date of payment specified in Paragraph 2, unless a contrary date is specified here:_____.

   In addition, the Sponsor shall provide the Designer with the following:

   (A) Tickets for travel, rental car, or other modes of transportation as follows: _____ _____

   (B) Food and lodging as follows: _____ _____

   (C) Other hospitality as follows: _____ _____

4. **Inability to Perform.** If the Designer is unable to appear on the dates scheduled in Paragraph 1 due to illness, the Sponsor shall have no obligation to make any payments under Paragraphs 2 and 3, but shall attempt to reschedule the Designer's appearance at a mutually acceptable future date. If the Sponsor is prevented from

having the Designer appear by Acts of God, hurricane, flood, governmental order, or other cause beyond its control, the Sponsor shall be responsible only for the payment of such expenses under Paragraph 3 as the Designer shall have actually incurred. The Sponsor agrees in such a case to attempt to reschedule the Designer's appearance at a mutually acceptable future date.

5. **Late Payment.** The Sponsor agrees that, in the event it is late in making payment of amounts due to the Designer under Paragraphs 2, 3, or 8, it will pay as additional liquidated damages _____ percent in interest on the amounts it is owing to the Designer, said interest to run from the date stipulated for payment in Paragraphs 2, 3, or 8 until such time as payment is made.

6. **Copyrights and Recordings.** Both parties agree that the Designer shall retain all rights, including copyrights, in relation to recordings of any kind made of the appearance or any works shown in the course thereof. The term "recording" as used herein shall include any recording made by electrical transcription, tape recording, wire recording, film, videotape, or other similar or dissimilar methods of recording, whether now known or hereinafter developed. No use of any such recording shall be made by the Sponsor without the written consent of the Designer and, if stipulated therein, additional compensation for such use.

7. **Insurance and Loss or Damage.** The Sponsor agrees that it shall provide wall-to-wall insurance for the works listed on the Schedule of Designs for the values specified therein. The Sponsor agrees that it shall be fully responsible and have strict liability for any loss or damage to the designs from the time said designs leaves the Designer's residence or studio until such time as it is returned there.

8. **Packing and Shipping.** The Sponsor agrees that it shall fully bear any costs of packing and shipping necessary to deliver the works specified in Paragraph 7 to the Sponsor and return them to the Designer's residence or studio.

9. **Modification.** This contract contains the full understanding between the parties hereto and may only be modified in a written instrument signed by both parties.

10. **Governing Law.** This contract shall be governed by the laws of the State of _____.

IN WITNESS WHEREOF, the parties hereto have signed this Agreement as of the date first set forth above.

Designer_____   Sponsor_____
                                                                    Company Name

                                             By_____
                                                                    Authorized Signatory, Title

Schedule of Designs

Title	Medium	Size	Value
1._____	_____	_____	_____
2._____	_____	_____	_____
3._____	_____	_____	_____
4._____	_____	_____	_____
5._____	_____	_____	_____
6._____	_____	_____	_____
7._____	_____	_____	_____

Licensing Contract to Merchandise Designs

AGREEMENT made this _____ day of _____, 19_____, between _____ (hereinafter referred to as the "Designer"), located at _____ and _____ (hereinafter referred to as the "Licensee"), located at _____ with respect to the use of a certain design created by the Designer (hereinafter referred to as the "Design") for manufactured products (hereinafter referred to as the "Licensed Products").

WHEREAS, the Designer is a professional designer of good standing; and

WHEREAS, the Designer has created the Design which the Designer wishes to license for purposes of manufacture and sale; and

WHEREAS, the Licensee wishes to use the Design to create a certain product or products for manufacture and sale; and

WHEREAS, both parties want to achieve the best possible quality to generate maximum sales;

NOW, THEREFORE, in consideration of the foregoing premises and the mutual covenants hereinafter set forth and other valuable consideration, the parties hereto agree as follows:

1. **Grant of Merchandising Rights.** The Designer grants to the Licensee the ❏ exclusive ❏ nonexclusive right to use the Design, titled _____ and described as _____, which was created and is owned by the Designer, as or as part of the following type(s) of merchandise:_____ _____ for manufacture, distribution, and sale by the Licensee in the following geographical area:_____ _____ and for the following period of time: _____.

2. **Ownership of Copyright.** The Designer shall retain all copyrights in and to the Design. The Licensee shall identify the Designer as the creator of the Design on the Licensed Products and shall reproduce thereon a copyright notice for the Designer which shall include the word "Copyright" or the symbol for copyright, the Designer's name, and the year date of first publication.

3. **Advance and Royalties.** Licensee agrees to pay Designer a nonrefundable advance in the amount of $_____ upon signing this Agreement, which advance shall be recouped from first royalties due hereunder. Licensee further agrees to pay Illustrator a royalty of _____ (_____ %) percent of the net sales of the Licensed Products. "Net Sales" as used herein shall mean sales to customers less prepaid freight and credits for lawful and customary volume rebates, actual returns, and allowances. Royalties shall be deemed to accrue when the Licensed Products are sold, shipped, or invoiced, whichever first occurs.

4. **Payments and Statements of Account.** Royalty payments shall be paid monthly on the first day of each month commencing _____, 19 _____, and Licensee shall with each payment furnish Designer with a monthly statement of account showing the kinds and quantities of all Licensed Products sold, the prices received therefor, and all deductions for freight, volume rebates, returns, and allowances. The Illustrator shall have the right to terminate this Agreement upon thirty (30) days notice if Licensee fails to make any payment required of it and does not cure this default within said thirty (30) days, whereupon all rights granted herein shall revert immediately to the Illustrator.

5. **Inspection of Books and Records.** Designer shall have the right to inspect Licensee's books and records concerning sales of the Licensed Products upon prior written notice.

6. Samples. Licensee shall give the Designer _____ samples of the Licensed Products for the Designer's personal use. The Designer shall have the right to purchase additional samples of the Licensed Products at the Licensee's manufacturing cost.

7. Quality of Reproductions. The Designer shall have the right to approve the quality of the reproduction of the Design on the Licensed Products, and the Designer agrees not to withhold approval unreasonably.

8. Promotion. Licensee shall use its best efforts to promote, distribute, and sell the Licensed Products.

9. Reservation of Rights. All rights not specifically transferred by this Agreement are reserved to the Designer.

10. Indemnification. The Licensee shall hold the Designer harmless from and against any loss, expense, or damage occasioned by any claim, demand, suit, or recovery against the Designer arising out of the use of the Image for the Licensed Products.

11. Assignment. Neither party shall assign rights or obligations under this Agreement, except that the Designer may assign the right to receive money due hereunder.

12. Nature of Contract. Nothing herein shall be construed to constitute the parties hereto joint venturers, nor shall any similar relationship be deemed to exist between them.

13. Governing Law. This Agreement shall be construed in accordance with the laws of _____; Licensee consents to the jurisdiction of the courts of _____.

14. Addresses. All notices, demands, payments, royalty payments, and statements shall be sent to the Designer at the following address _____ and to the Licensee at _____.

15. Modifications in Writing. This Agreement constitutes the entire agreement between the parties hereto and shall not be modified, amended, or changed in any way except by a written agreement signed by both parties hereto.

IN WITNESS WHEREOF, the parties have signed this Agreement as of the date first set forth above.

Designer_____   Licensee_____
              Company Name   Company Name

By_____   By_____
      Authorized Signatory, Title   Authorized Signatory, Title

Release Form for Models

In consideration of _____ Dollars ($_____), receipt of which is acknowledged, I, _____, do hereby give _____, his or her assigns, licensees, and legal representatives the irrevocable right to use my name (or any fictional name), picture, portrait, or photograph in all forms and media and in all manners, including composite or distorted representations, for advertising, trade, or any other lawful purposes, and I waive any right to inspect or approve the finished version(s), including written copy that may be created in connection therewith. I am of full age.* I have read this release and am fully familiar with its contents.

Witness_____   Model_____

Address_____   Address_____

Date _____, 19 ___

————————————————————— Consent (if applicable) —————————————————————

I am the parent or guardian of the minor named above and have the legal authority to execute the above release. I approve the foregoing and waive any rights in the premises.

Witness_____   Parent or Guardian_____

Address_____   Address_____

Date _____, 19 ___

* Delete this sentence if the subject is a minor. The parent or guardian must then sign the consent.

Property Release

In consideration of the sum of _____ Dollars ($_____),

receipt of which is hereby acknowledged, I, _____,

located at _____, do irrevocably authorize

_____, his or her assigns, licensees, heirs, and legal representatives, to copyright, publish, and use in all forms and media and in all manners for advertising, trade, or any other lawful purpose, images of the following property which I own and have full and sole authority to license for such uses: _____

_____,

regardless of whether said use is composite or distorted in character or form, whether said use is made in conjunction with my own name or with a fictitious name, or whether said use is made in color or otherwise or other derivative works are made through any medium.

I waive any right that I may have to inspect or approve the finished version(s), including written copy that may be used in connection therewith.

I am of full age and have every right to contract in my own name with respect to the foregoing matters. I have read the above authorization and release prior to its execution and I am fully cognizant of its contents.

Witness_____   Owner_____

Address_____   Date_____,19_____

Permission Form

The Undersigned hereby grant(s) permission to _____ (hereinafter referred to as the "Designer"), located at _____, and to the Designer's successors and assigns, to use the material specified in this Permission Form for the following book or other product _____ for use by the following publisher or client _____.

This permission is for the following material:

Nature of material _____

Source _____

Exact description of material, including page numbers_____

        If published, date of publication _____

        Publisher _____

        Author(s) _____

This material may be used for the book or product named above and in any future revisions, derivations, or editions thereof, including nonexclusive world rights in all languages.

It is understood that the grant of this permission shall in no way restrict republication of the material by the Undersigned or others authorized by the Undersigned.

If specified here, the material shall be accompanied on publication by a copyright notice as follows_____ _____

and a credit line as follows _____.

Other provisions, if any: _____

If specified here, the requested rights are not controlled in their entirety by the Undersigned and the following owners must be contacted: _____ _____

One copy of this Permission Form shall be returned to the Designer and one copy shall be retained by the Undersigned.

_____   _____
Authorized Signatory   Date

_____   _____
Authorized Signatory   Date

Nondisclosure Agreement for Submitting Ideas

AGREEMENT, entered into as of this _____ day of _____, 19___, between_____ (hereinafter referred to as the "Designer"), located at _____, and _____ (hereinafter referred to as the "Recipient"), located at _____.

WHEREAS, the Designer has developed certain valuable information, concepts, ideas, or designs, which the Designer deems confidential (hereinafter referred to as the "Information"); and

WHEREAS, the Recipient is in the business of using such Information for its projects and wishes to review the Information; and

WHEREAS, the Designer wishes to disclose this Information to the Recipient; and

WHEREAS, the Recipient is willing not to disclose this Information, as provided in this Agreement.

NOW, THEREFORE, in consideration of the foregoing premises and the mutual covenants hereinafter set forth and other valuable considerations, the parties hereto agree as follows:

1. **Disclosure.** Designer shall disclose to the Recipient the Information, which concerns:_____
_____

2. **Purpose.** Recipient agrees that this disclosure is only for the purpose of the Recipient's evaluation to determine its interest in the commercial exploitation of the Information.

3. **Limitation on Use.** Recipient agrees not to manufacture, sell, deal in, or otherwise use or appropriate the disclosed Information in any way whatsoever, including but not limited to adaptation, imitation, redesign, or modification. Nothing contained in this Agreement shall be deemed to give Recipient any rights whatsoever in and to the Information.

4. **Confidentiality.** Recipient understands and agrees that the unauthorized disclosure of the Information by the Recipient to others would irreparably damage the Designer. As consideration and in return for the disclosure of this Information, the Recipient shall keep secret and hold in confidence all such Information and treat the Information as if it were the Recipient's own proprietary property by not disclosing it to any person or entity.

5. **Good Faith Negotiations.** If, on the basis of the evaluation of the Information, Recipient wishes to pursue the exploitation thereof, Recipient agrees to enter into good faith negotiations to arrive at a mutually satisfactory agreement for these purposes. Until and unless such an agreement is entered into, this nondisclosure Agreement shall remain in force.

6. **Miscellany.** This Agreement shall be binding upon and shall inure to the benefit of the parties and their respective legal representatives, successors, and assigns.

IN WITNESS WHEREOF, the parties have signed this Agreement as of the date first set forth above.

Designer_____   Recipient_____
                                                                       Company Name

                                                                   By_____
                                                                       Authorized Signatory, Title

Copyright Transfer Form

FOR VALUABLE CONSIDERATION, the receipt of which is hereby acknowledged, _____

(hereinafter referred to as the "Assignor"), located at _____,

does hereby transfer and assign to _____, located

at _____, his or her heirs, executors, administrators,

and assigns, the following rights: _____

_____ in the copyrights

in the works described as follows:

Title	Registration Number	Nature of Work
_____	_____	_____
_____	_____	_____
_____	_____	_____
_____	_____	_____
_____	_____	_____

IN WITNESS WHEREOF, the Assignor has executed this instrument on the _____ day of _____, 19___.

Assignor_____

FORM VA
UNITED STATES COPYRIGHT OFFICE

REGISTRATION NUMBER

_____

VA   VAU

EFFECTIVE DATE OF REGISTRATION

_____
Month   Day   Year

DO NOT WRITE ABOVE THIS LINE. IF YOU NEED MORE SPACE, USE A SEPARATE CONTINUATION SHEET.

1

TITLE OF THIS WORK ▼

NATURE OF THIS WORK ▼ See instructions

PREVIOUS OR ALTERNATIVE TITLES ▼

PUBLICATION AS A CONTRIBUTION   If this work was published as a contribution to a periodical, serial, or collection, give information about the collective work in which the contribution appeared.   **Title of Collective Work ▼**

If published in a periodical or serial give: **Volume ▼**   **Number ▼**   **Issue Date ▼**   **On Pages ▼**

2

NOTE

Under the law, the "author" of a "work made for hire" is generally the employer, not the employee (see instructions). For any part of this work that was "made for hire" check "Yes" in the space provided, give the employer (or other person for whom the work was prepared) as "Author" of that part, and leave the space for dates of birth and death blank.

a

NAME OF AUTHOR ▼

DATES OF BIRTH AND DEATH
Year Born ▼   Year Died ▼

Was this contribution to the work a "work made for hire"?
☐ Yes
☐ No

AUTHOR'S NATIONALITY OR DOMICILE
Name of Country
OR { Citizen of ▶_____
      Domiciled in ▶_____

WAS THIS AUTHOR'S CONTRIBUTION TO THE WORK
Anonymous?   ☐ Yes ☐ No
Pseudonymous? ☐ Yes ☐ No
If the answer to either of these questions is "Yes," see detailed instructions.

NATURE OF AUTHORSHIP   Briefly describe nature of the material created by this author in which copyright is claimed. ▼

b

NAME OF AUTHOR ▼

DATES OF BIRTH AND DEATH
Year Born ▼   Year Died ▼

Was this contribution to the work a "work made for hire"?
☐ Yes
☐ No

AUTHOR'S NATIONALITY OR DOMICILE
Name of country
OR { Citizen of ▶_____
      Domiciled in ▶_____

WAS THIS AUTHOR'S CONTRIBUTION TO THE WORK
Anonymous?   ☐ Yes ☐ No
Pseudonymous? ☐ Yes ☐ No
If the answer to either of these questions is "Yes," see detailed instructions.

NATURE OF AUTHORSHIP   Briefly describe nature of the material created by this author in which copyright is claimed. ▼

c

NAME OF AUTHOR ▼

DATES OF BIRTH AND DEATH
Year Born ▼   Year Died ▼

Was this contribution to the work a "work made for hire"?
☐ Yes
☐ No

AUTHOR'S NATIONALITY OR DOMICILE
Name of Country
OR { Citizen of ▶_____
      Domiciled in ▶_____

WAS THIS AUTHOR'S CONTRIBUTION TO THE WORK
Anonymous?   ☐ Yes ☐ No
Pseudonymous? ☐ Yes ☐ No
If the answer to either of these questions is "Yes," see detailed instructions.

NATURE OF AUTHORSHIP   Briefly describe nature of the material created by this author in which copyright is claimed. ▼

3

a YEAR IN WHICH CREATION OF THIS WORK WAS COMPLETED   This information must be given in all cases.
◀ Year

b DATE AND NATION OF FIRST PUBLICATION OF THIS PARTICULAR WORK   Complete this information ONLY if this work has been published.
Month ▶ _____ Day ▶ _____ Year ▶ _____
◀ Nation

4

See instructions before completing this space.

COPYRIGHT CLAIMANT(S) Name and address must be given even if the claimant is the same as the author given in space 2.▼

TRANSFER If the claimant(s) named here in space 4 are different from the author(s) named in space 2, give a brief statement of how the claimant(s) obtained ownership of the copyright.▼

DO NOT WRITE HERE
OFFICE USE ONLY

APPLICATION RECEIVED
_____

ONE DEPOSIT RECEIVED
_____

TWO DEPOSITS RECEIVED
_____

REMITTANCE NUMBER AND DATE
_____

MORE ON BACK ▶   • Complete all applicable spaces (numbers 5-9) on the reverse side of this page.
• See detailed instructions.   • Sign the form at line 8.

DO NOT WRITE HERE

Page 1 of _____ pages

DO NOT WRITE ABOVE THIS LINE. IF YOU NEED MORE SPACE, USE A SEPARATE CONTINUATION SHEET.

PREVIOUS REGISTRATION Has registration for this work, or for an earlier version of this work, already been made in the Copyright Office?

☐ **Yes** ☐ **No** If your answer is "Yes," why is another registration being sought? (Check appropriate box) ▼

☐ This is the first published edition of a work previously registered in unpublished form.

☐ This is the first application submitted by this author as copyright claimant.

☐ This is a changed version of the work, as shown by space 6 on this application.

If your answer is "Yes," give: **Previous Registration Number** ▼　　　　**Year of Registration** ▼

5

DERIVATIVE WORK OR COMPILATION Complete both space 6a & 6b for a derivative work; complete only 6b for a compilation.

a. Preexisting Material Identify any preexisting work or works that this work is based on or incorporates. ▼

b. Material Added to This Work Give a brief, general statement of the material that has been added to this work and in which copyright is claimed.▼

6

See instructions before completing this space

DEPOSIT ACCOUNT If the registration fee is to be charged to a Deposit Account established in the Copyright Office, give name and number of Account.

Name ▼　　　　**Account Number** ▼

7

CORRESPONDENCE Give name and address to which correspondence about this application should be sent.　Name/Address/Apt/City/State/Zip ▼

Area Code & Telephone Number ▶

Be sure to give your daytime phone ◀ number.

CERTIFICATION* I, the undersigned, hereby certify that I am the

Check only one ▼

☐ author

☐ other copyright claimant

☐ owner of exclusive right(s)

☐ authorized agent of⎯⎯⎯⎯⎯⎯⎯⎯⎯⎯⎯⎯⎯⎯⎯⎯⎯⎯⎯⎯
　　　　　　　　Name of author or other copyright claimant, or owner of exclusive right(s) ▲

8

of the work identified in this application and that the statements made
by me in this application are correct to the best of my knowledge.

Typed or printed name and date ▼ If this application gives a date of publication in space 3, do not sign and submit it before that date.

⎯⎯⎯⎯⎯⎯⎯⎯⎯⎯⎯⎯⎯⎯⎯⎯⎯⎯⎯⎯⎯⎯⎯⎯⎯⎯⎯⎯⎯ **date ▶** ⎯⎯⎯⎯⎯⎯⎯⎯⎯⎯⎯

Handwritten signature (X) ▼

MAIL CERTIFICATE TO

Certificate will be mailed in window envelope

Name ▼

Number/Street/Apartment Number ▼

City/State/ZIP ▼

9

* 17 U.S.C. § 506(e) Any person who knowingly makes a false representation of a material fact in the application for copyright registration provided for by section 409, or in any written statement filed in connection with the application, shall be fined not more than $2,500.

June 1989—100,000　　　　　　　　　　　　　　　　　　　　U.S. GOVERNMENT PRINTING OFFICE: 1989—241-428/80,02

Index